*For Larry
who was with me
at the beginning
with affection.
Irene
3/1/10*

# ENCOUNTERS

## A Book of Memories

Irene Mahoney, O.S.U.

*AuthorHouse*™
*1663 Liberty Drive*
*Bloomington, IN 47403*
*www.authorhouse.com*
*Phone: 1-800-839-8640*

© *2010 Irene Mahoney, O.S.U. All rights reserved.*

*No part of this book may be reproduced, stored in a retrieval system, or transmitted by any means without the written permission of the author.*

*First published by AuthorHouse 1/20/2010*

*ISBN: 978-1-4490-7677-1 (e)*
*ISBN: 978-1-4490-7687-0 (sc)*

*Library of Congress Control Number: 2010900498*

*Printed in the United States of America*
*Bloomington, Indiana*

*This book is printed on acid-free paper.*

# OTHER BOOKS BY IRENE MAHONEY

Marie of the Incarnation: Mystic and Missionary

Royal Cousin: The Life of Henri of Navarre

Madame Catherine: The Life of Catherine de Medici

Seven Sons

Accidental Grace

Marie of the Incarnation: Selected Writings

Far From Home

A Company of Women

Swatow: Ursulines in China

A Far Country

Lady Blackrobes

## PLAYS

Portraits Of Angela

All That I Am

Not By Half

Off With Their Heads

For Nancy

*Our friendship is made
Of being awake.*

Rumi

Whether at once, as once at a crash Paul
Or as Austen, a lingering-out sweet skill,
Make mercy in all of us, out of us all
Mastery, but be adored, but be adored King.


*Gerard Manley Hopkins*

ENCOUNTERS

## CONTENTS

| | |
|---|---|
| *Foreword* | ix |
| *Introduction* | xi |
| The Story Man | 1 |
| Keeping the Light | 13 |
| Mazda and Jane | 21 |
| The Writing Life I | 29 |
| Finding My Voice | 39 |
| A Writer's Diary | 49 |
| The Writing Life II | 61 |
| Walking to Cathay | 71 |
| To Climb a Mountain | 77 |
| Swatches from a Taiwan Diary | 85 |
| Practicing the Great Resolve | 95 |
| Buddhist Nun and the "Holy Father" | 107 |
| Homecoming | 117 |
| Nova Nada Journal | 129 |
| Seeing in the Dark | 149 |
| Learning God | 159 |

# ENCOUNTERS

## **FOREWORD**

"As long as she could remember, God had been part of her consciousness . . . . He was loving, compassionate, and understood her completely. If she was alien with the rest of the world, she was totally at ease with God. All the man-made rules of religion had nothing to do with God. He belonged to her without restraint." So wrote Irene Mahoney in an autobiographical essay, "Turning Toward the Light," published in *A Company of Women*.

This is as good a summary of the meaning of contemplation as one can find. Contemplation, one might say, is a habit of being, a haunting awareness of God's presence. A contemplative life demands risk – rather like an entrance into the desert, where all the comfortable thoughts and words and images of God are given up or taken away, so that God may give us Himself. As C.S. Lewis wrote, "Each image of Him that we form, He must in mercy shatter."

What then is the connection between contemplation and the life of the writer? First of all, the contemplative, like the writer, engages in a constant search for meaning: how to be, how to be more deeply, and how to express this mystery in words. The story that is history, the cycle of humanity's tale, the saga of human experience – it all leaves the writer and the contemplative stunned, sometimes radiantly happy, sometimes mute with grief. This state of wonder at beholding the depth of things is the point at which the contemplative becomes a writer, and where the writer contemplates.

This is the world of contemplative writers among whom is Irene Mahoney. These are those who have first been found by God and who have responded; precisely because of their openness to grace, they somehow find the right words, the telling words that leave us breathless. This, for example, is the experience Irene describes in her novel *An Accidental Grace*, when a character returns to a convent that seems on the verge of dissolution:

> For a second, in a sudden intake of breath, Ruth felt a shock like lightning. Her darkness was riven, and for an instant she was able to affirm the presence of light – not only for herself, but for all of them struggling out of darkness. When she looked up, the moment of transparency had passed. They looked no different from before. Yet the very heart of their dedication had been touched. For a moment what had worn the mask of death had been transfigured with life.

In her historical biographies and richly imagined novels, in her compelling plays, and her reflective essays, Irene Mahoney has turned a penetrating light where often there is only darkness. With *Encounters* there is light again but this time not simply as characters from history or from her imagination but from her own life. *Encounters*, as she tells us, is a Book of Memories drawn from her own rich and diverse experience.

Donald Spoto
Sjælland, Denmark

# ENCOUNTERS

# INTRODUCTION

*We must wait until evening*
*Before we see how lovely the day has been*

Sophocles

Despite my passionate avowals to the contrary, with *Encounters* I have written a memoir. It is not chronological nor is it complete but it is a book of reflective memories – memories which rise up with startling resonance despite the blur of time.

Most of my adult life has been spent as a consecrated religious woman. It was, as I have been told more than once, an odd choice for me to have made. From the beginning I was considered an unlikely candidate – both by those who made the choices and even by myself. By background and temperament I was, as the expression goes, "outside the box." God, however, who is basically the Chooser in such affairs, thought otherwise.

In addition to all the logical reasons why I would not "fit," there was an unexamined reason which even I recognized as a serious obstacle. Long before I thought of a life of consecration to God I had imaged my life as a writer. To be a writer, as I conceived it, was more than a profession. It was in every sense a vocation. Even I recognized that one could hardly pursue two vocations. "You cannot love God and Mammon," it said in the Gospel. Clearly writing was my Mammon. While God, I recognize now, would have been more broadminded, religious life in the days before Vatican II had little room for the Nun-as-Writer.

The young Gerard Manley Hopkins had looked at both vocations and felt that their demands were such that one must choose one over the other – although his later life does not bear out this decision. The later writer, Thomas Merton, assisted by a hundred years of psychology, comes closer to present day reality: "It is possible to doubt whether I have become a monk, but it is not possible to doubt that I am a writer, that I was born and will most probably die one." It took me more than half a lifetime to understand and agree with Merton's conclusion. Being a writer was the most fundamental element of my being. Even if I could change my nationality, my color, my sex, there was no way that I could annul my vocation as a writer. Could I at the same time be faithful to this vocation and to the life of consecration to God?

When I began to plan *Encounters* I had no "theme" to guide me. I saw it as a book of reflective essays ranging widely over a long and far-reaching life. I had been an editor at a New York publishing company, I had been a professor in a college in Westchester County, I had been an English teacher

# ENCOUNTERS

in a language college in Taiwan, I had traveled widely – to China, Thailand, Australia. And in the last segment of my life I had, at last, been a writer. Through it all I had been a member of the Order of St. Ursula.

In the months I sat reflecting on the topics which might become part of *Encounters*, it became increasingly clear that what had absorbed me throughout my adult life was this insistent double vocation I had struggled to live for over sixty years. As I winnowed down the list, I was surprised, however, by how many of these images came from my childhood. Although my first tendency was to discard them as not relevant to my basic theme, yet as I examined them more closely I recognized in them those essential qualities of a writer: memory and imagination. Even as a child I had been absorbed by the act of writing. From the beginning I had been aware of the cadences of speech, watched the subtle shifts of expression, remembered the narrative movements of an event. Now all these stored images came rising up out of something deeper even than memory.

The wonder was that everything "fit." The images of "God" and "Mammon" with which I had wrestled for years had slipped away – one as false as the other. There was no need to choose. It was all one, as I was one.

The writer and the nun: some watercolors, some pencil sketches, a pastel or two. Images of a life.

*Feast of Pentecost*
*May 31, 2009*

# ENCOUNTERS

# THE STORY MAN

My father, unlike my mother, was a letter writer. Through my boarding school years and later into college there was always a weekly letter. But the only letter that remains from his correspondence is not to me but to my half-sister Peggy. Peg was at that time about twelve, the youngest of the six children who had lost their mother several years before. At the date of the letter (August 23, 1917) she was on vacation with her older sister Mary, soon to be married.

"My dear little Peggy," the letter begins. It is a letter of both affection and humor. He had a terrible time, he describes to her in detail, with the Italian lady at the vegetable store who was trying to sell him small inferior potatoes. But he won in the end getting the big ones he and Peggy both like. And what a dream he had! His Peggy came riding down Pine St. on a big cow, hanging on for dear life. It was an image he knew would make her laugh. But the tone, the tone throughout, is one of such transparent affection that it suffuses everything else.

He hopes, he continues, that she is having a good time but not so good that she will forget him. He waits for her letters and is disappointed when he waits in vain. But even this is said not with chiding but with a kind of whimsy, certain of their mutual affection. He is writing at the end of the day. He has just finished changing the beds and cleaning the dining room. He is tired but not so tired that he would put off writing to her. Had she been home, she would have been working with him – his faithful little helper. But now he is going to bed. Maybe he will try to go to see her brother Joe on Sunday but he's not sure if that will work out. "And so I close," he writes, "Saying Goodbye, Little Sweetheart, with best wishes, Pop."

The letters my father wrote to me had a different ring. It was a different time. The anxiety of his widowed years was over. The children were grown with children of their own. He was older now and settled with a good job and a devoted wife who had given him a girl-child despite the peril to her own life. The child was his Benjamin whom he loved as a treasure beyond his expectations.

When I was in my novel-writing mode I had written a long semi-autobiographical novel called *Solo Voices*. Each part was seen from the viewpoint of a different narrator: the motherless child, the second wife, the child of the second marriage. The whole production, I have come to realize, was a passionate endeavor to understand those relationships and come to terms with them. I know now that my goal was beyond my reach. I will never really understand. Even now I still see myself as that bewildered child trying to grasp the reaches of my father's life so far beyond the boundaries of my own.

The father I knew was in his sixties but he was one of those people classified as "young of heart." A job, a house, a wife were the elements which kept him faithful and domesticated. But beyond them were the dreams he could never relinquish – dreams of a world beyond, a world of color and excitement – and fantasy. And the memories – memories which he kept as part of his secret life. "What are you thinking about?" my mother would ask when she came across him leaning back in the porch recliner, his eyes half closed. He never told her, of course; it would have taken too long to bring the long trail of memories and dreams into the present. And she never waited.

When I was a little older we would sometimes take long walks in the summer evenings. When we came home, picking our way along the dirt road illumined by the moon, my mother would ask, "What were you talking about with your father?" "Nothing," I would reply with the maddening secrecy of adolescence. But in fact it was true. We did not talk much. It was another kind of discourse that we had. He opened the way into his silence and enabled me to share it.

I don't know how old my father was when he was first married. Young, certainly. Probably too young. He was sixteen when he came over from Ireland. Perhaps he was motivated by a sense of responsibility to get a job in the Golden Country and "help out" those he had "left behind." But I rather doubt it. At sixteen he was moved more by adventure than responsibility. Crossing the ocean was a "bit of a lark." Although he had no close relatives waiting for him, his buoyancy was willing to trust fate and the help of the lads who had gone over before him. Later he described himself as a "strapping omadhoun" and this was probably close to the truth. Big, fearless and wonderfully engaging, he joined himself to a group of fellow immigrants who helped him along – just as he had predicted. He found a job and, in short time, a wife.

I have tried a million times to image Julia Morrissey, known in the family as "Curly" for her mass of red hair. I have hunted for old photos of her but although I have unearthed photos of my father in a 1900s bathing suit preening himself at Coney Island, I have never found an image of Curly. Hints here and there have pictured her as young, pretty and irrepressible. She was a singer, a dancer, a player of the jew's-harp – and the mother of six children. She could not have been more than mid-thirties when the first signs of kidney disease appeared. For the next few years her four sons and two daughters grew up in a household where their mother was sometimes in hospital, often in bed, and always distanced from them by her increasing inability to share their lives.

Those were the years that shaped the dark wordless memories which I sometimes felt on the evening walks with my father. When she died he was left with a family beyond his control. The most he could do was to take a second job in an effort to pay the mountain of medical bills and the mortgage payments. Years later I heard my aunt commenting on those days, "Poor Florrie, all he could do was try to keep a roof over their heads." The boys, in their adolescence, were aimless in a world that had never given them parameters. They tore up the warning notices that came from their schools and when the truant officer arrived he found an empty house with the doors invitingly unlocked. When Mary, the older of the girls, announced that she was getting married, her father was relieved.

His life was centered on the only child he could still reach. Peggy could not have been more than nine when her mother died. She had become a practical and independent child – the one who was home to help with the laundry, to fix tea for her mother after school. Now she had lost even that role. Mary was out with her beau and the boys were in the cellar with their friends telling jokes she couldn't understand. Pop was home so little that she scarcely knew him but then one day in her desperation she burrowed into his arms and he wrapped her in his own loneliness. What none of the others seemed to need he offered to Peggy.

For the next three years they lived together like that. Mary had her own home and one by one the boys drifted away. There were just Peggy and Pop, rattling around in their ramshackle house. Then he met Mary Rourke – not at a wedding but at a funeral. I have a picture taken around that time of the woman who would become my mother. Sometimes as I was growing up, I studied it trying to find something of my stocky body in her tall willowy frame with her ink-black hair piled on her head in abundance. It was an image of a poised and resolute woman. It was years before I was able to see the fear and uncertainty beneath that façade.

Certainly there was every reason to be fearful when she committed herself in marriage to Florrie O'Mahoney. He was close to fifty and she forty-two when they were married. Her age would ordinarily win her the label of spinster – very close to the hushed designation of Old Maid. But Mary Rourke escaped the labels. She had not stayed home to mind the house or take care of aged parents. She had been a "business woman" in an era when such a vocation was considered close to eccentric. The kindest response of Florrie's relatives and friends was amazement. Why, they gossiped, would such a lady want to marry poor Florrie with his children and his debts? And him only a New York cop? Of the children, the three oldest, well off on their own, were satisfied with expressing their disdain of this cool reserved woman with her "fancy ways." The three youngest, locked in the bonds of this new and unexpected household, responded with full adolescent rancor.

Those who were willing to give the marriage a chance conceded that poor Florrie needed a woman to help with the children, to keep the house in order, to fix the meals. He needed what they called "a helpmate." But Florrie O'Mahoney had not sought a helpmate; he had sought no one. The thing was that something strange had fallen upon him. At the moment he could least expect it, he had fallen in love.

In all the years they were married his love never diminished. In the antagonistic years of my adolescence I was fiercely jealous of that love. I was jealous of the look on my father's face as he watched my mother – always graceful, always poised – walk downstairs in the fur coat he had bought her with such prideful devotion. He would give her anything, but she asked for very little. Even his affection, overt and spontaneous, sometimes seemed more than she needed. It took almost half a lifetime for me to recognize that their love was reciprocal, that my mother loved this guileless, upright man with a resolute devotion to protect him from a world too clever for his innocence. After his death I tried to ask her one day about their relationship – how they had met, when she knew she was falling in love, when she decided to marry this unlikely suitor; but even such innocent questions invaded her privacy. She turned away, blinking back the tears. "I thought he had the look of a saint," was all she said.

# ENCOUNTERS

But for all that there was a chasm between them – the unshared life of my father's past. I remember the first time I heard in church the Gospel about the woman whose husband died and who, according to Jewish tradition, married his brothers one after another. "In the Resurrection," the passage concluded, "whose wife will she be?"

The question terrified me. What would happen to my mother and me on the Last Day? Would my father return to his first wife and their children? Would we be cast out into some nether world? In some form or other the question was always there: the question of this former life, kept secret from us, where this man I had learned to call "Daddy" had been called "Pop" by six other children whom he had also begotten and loved.

Our move from New York City to the north shore of Long Island was a dramatic event which changed our lives. For my father it was a fortuitous move offering him a job which raised his status and moved him to a country environment which he loved. For my mother it was a wrenching change which divested her of her home, her family, her friends. She did it without complaint but it seems to me now as I reflect on those years that she never again fully reclaimed her life.

I already knew my father as a supreme story-teller. Despite his limited education he was a repository of Irish tales and legends. Long before I was able to read I knew about the Irish giants and the Little Green Man with the Little Red Pocketbook with his limitless help for those in need. But even more engaging were the tales my father constructed from his imagination. There was the story of how when he was first courting my mother, he, like the great heroes of Ireland, had saved her from death. They were crossing an avenue, he recounted, when the heel of her shoe caught in the trolley tracks. He leaned down to pull it out but to no avail. He finally (gently and reverently) lifted her foot out of the shoe while she put her arm around his shoulders for balance. (Oh the joy of it to feel her body pressed against him and the slender foot in his hands!) But the shoe remained hopelessly stuck. As he looked up he saw the trolley bearing down upon them. What could he do but pick her up – leaving the shoe behind – and carry her across the dangerous intersection to safety! I glowed with the joy of it all, the more so as my mother, unsmiling, denied that it had ever happened.

That was my second favorite story. The first – of course – was about me. And once again my father was the hero. When he first looked upon me in the hospital, he recounted, he knew he was looking at the most beautiful baby God had ever made and he knew he wasn't alone – all around him the doctors and nurses stood, eyes wide at this glorious child. When it was time to take me home, he continued, he was wheeling my mother out of the hospital while she held the baby carefully in her lap. And then from nowhere appeared a man who knocked my father down and snatched the baby from its mother's arms. He staggered to his feet just in time to see the man turn the corner running for "dear life" – his favorite expression – with his precious burden. He caught just a glimpse of his face, dark and scowling, with a black mustache. The mustache was the perfect touch. In every rendition, I grew shivery with delight at the mention of that Mustache. Of course, I knew what was coming. Nothing could keep my heroic father from recovering his beautiful child. Down the streets he ran, knocking people out of the way, fighting with the policeman who tried to stop him, never losing sight of the dark man with the Mustache. They crossed avenues just ahead of oncoming street cars. He even grabbed a skate board from a bewildered kid so he could make faster headway. It was a glorious chase which left me breathless. Of course in the end he caught up with the Mustache and snatched his precious baby to safety. It was a parable of love which shaped my heart.

By the time of our Long Island years the older children were married with families of their own. Occasionally a couple of them would arrive with their children over the weekend but they were never comfortable in our house. Sometimes they would meet my father somewhere else or go down to the beach for a picnic, arriving back at sunset just in time to say goodbye before starting the trek back to New York.

I hated those days, caught between a feeling of loyalty to my mother and the half-acknowledged longing to join this group of sandy-haired, blue-eyed people – so different from me – who shared my blood. As far as I remember we never spoke of these visits. My mother was tight-lipped and angular after everyone had left. My father was silent. The miracle is that the love between them, mute and constrained after these encounters, was strong enough to span the chasm.

When I was twenty-one and my father seventy-two, I told him that I had decided to enter an order of cloistered nuns. From one perspective, it was an act of inexcusable cruelty, but that was a perspective to which I was blinded by the exalted vision of giving my life to God. Unlike my mother, he had nothing but respect for the course I was anticipating. He wept for the sheer anguish of losing the child he had once snatched at risk of life and limb from the dark man with the black mustache.

I saw my father very little in the next six years. When finally I made my solemn life commitment he was already suffering from severe heart problems. Less than a year later he died. My mother called me early on a Saturday morning to give me the news. It was a bad connection in every way. The rule of my Order did not permit me to be there at his death. He died at home as he wished. My mother took care of him despite her own frailty. He asked her once to lie with him in his bed, "for comfort," he explained, trying to dissipate her shock. It was the first time since my conception that they had shared a bed. She could not risk another pregnancy and their religion did not permit birth control.

At the end Peggy arrived – the little girl he had written to so long before, his letter telling her how much he missed her and ending , "And so I close, saying goodbye, Little Sweetheart." I don't know much about the funeral. Cloister is an effective device for exile. My mother came to see me several weeks later but she said little. The black dress, the pale, drawn face, the nervous hands restrained my questions. At the time I felt no need to know more. The only thing that mattered was that my father was dead and that I had not been there. That was all I needed to know. It was grief enough.

Later, of course, I wondered about the funeral. I supposed all the children were there. Were his sons pall bearers: Johnny, Tom, Francis, Joe? Was Mary, the oldest, there with her successful businessman husband and her two married children? And Peggy – separated now with two children, living a hard-scrabble life with an off-and-on alcoholic husband. She was there, of course. And my mother. At the last had they found a way of addressing her with respect? Finally: this man with the "face of a saint" who had held us together and kept us apart, dead now but still at the center of the story.

It was a great story he had lived. I shared so little that I can only guess at most of it. Even in death his silences remain. I cherish the evening walks we took, when I felt I had entered into something of his silence. I rejoice in his mythic stories that burst forth so effortlessly, so full of his own delight in telling them. That tumble of words has been his legacy to me. In trying to capture him, I know I should begin, "Once upon a time . . . ."

ENCOUNTERS

# KEEPING THE LIGHT

    I spent my sixth birthday in our big brownstone house in Brooklyn. Almost immediately after that we moved to Long Island. I don't remember much about the move except that the butcher had given me a cat and since we were moving to the "country" my mother said we could keep it. Despite my father's joyful assurances that living in the country was going to be a wonderful experience, I found the country frightening. I missed the orderly streets with their curbs and sidewalks and traffic lights to give you signals for walking and stopping. The birds, too, were frightening, far different from the small "chippies" my father and I had fed on Sunday mornings in Prospect Park. These were huge birds, black and intimidating with their ugly, strident voices. Crows, my father named them, assuring me that they wouldn't hurt me.

    Three months after we arrived I began school. Instead of being a three-block walk around the corner from our house, "school" was a car-ride away. My father drove me in his police car; I took my lunch in a tin box which had a place for a thermos. In the afternoon he picked me up and drove me home.

I have no idea how many children there were in my class but to an only child anything more than three seems like a crowd. "Do you live on a farm?" asked a first grade classmate who always seemed to smell of potatoes. "I guess so," I said, not quite sure what a farm was. Most of the children did live on farms, I learned; this was potato and cauliflower country. We however, had our modest house in "estate country" where my father was "captain" of the single-man police force.

In time I grew used to the two-lane roads with no sidewalks to provide safety for pedestrians; I grew used to having no neighboring houses, no playmates, no vegetable markets or meat markets where the friendly butcher sometimes would offer you a piece of bologna as a treat. My father became my best playmate and when he was off-duty we explored the narrow roads or investigated the bridle paths which laced the surrounding woods. The best walk of all was straight up our road, turning left at the end until you found yourself with a body of water on your right. Old Field, the residential village where we lived, was built on a spit of land jutting into Long Island Sound. On one side lay the choppy waters of the Sound and on the other the placid waters of Conscience Bay. If you kept walking, as we almost always did, you came to the confluence of the waters. You were on high ground here, with a steep cliff descending into a rocky headland. In time, after a number of adventuresome boys had tumbled down with broken bones to prove it, a restraining fence was built. But as I remember it the grass extended straight to the edge of the cliff without impediment. This was where I got my greatest thrill, stretching my foot until I could feel the earth give way beneath my toes while I clutched my father's hand.

Over to the right, set back from the cliff, was a large stone house with a tower topped by what looked to me like a very large glass bowl. This was Old Field Light, providing the beacon which guided ships away from the rocky beach. My father, with a capacity for knowing everyone, knew the lighthouse keeper and sometimes on a Saturday afternoon we would go and talk to him. He was a small man, lean, abrupt in his movements with grizzled hair and eyes that crinkled shut against the light. Sometimes we went into his house, sitting in the kitchen while Mr. Ray boiled water for tea. On nice days I wandered in the little park, listening to the waves breaking against the rocks and scrupulously avoiding the danger of the cliff. On cold days I sat and listened while the men talked.

My father was a talker, his slight Irish lilt turning everything into a bardic narrative. But Mr. Ray was a man of few words. What he said came out in spurts, ragged and disconnected, but all the more intriguing for being so hard to catch. His talk was often about the shoreline and how it had shifted, about rich folk buying up property along the Sound and destroying the beach. Sometimes there was mention of a fishing boat lost in a sudden squall. To this my father would shake his head, "Poor sods," he would say, "I suppose they never had a chance." And Mr. Ray would nod. "The sea's not easy," he'd say, "not easy."

It was on afternoons like this while the men talked and I amused myself with Mr. Ray's rock collection, neatly displayed on the wide window sills that surrounded the kitchen, that I learned about Mr. Ray's wife, Adela, and Middle Ground Light. When they were first married they continued to live far out on the South Fork near where they had grown up. As a young man he worked as a seaman but their hope was to save enough money to buy a little farm and raise their family. It was hard times, though, in the Depression and they couldn't get the loan they needed. When he was offered a job as lighthouse keeper he jumped at it, although it meant moving across the Island to the North Shore. "Adela, she didn't seem to mind," he explained, but that was before they knew it was Middle Ground Light they were offered.

Middle Ground Light was situated on a shoal that ran for three-quarters of a mile in the waters that separated Connecticut from the northern shore of Long Island. The structure that rose out of the water was a feat of architecture: a Gothic Revival building, two stories high, with an octagonal tower rising at its side. It's a wonder how when it was built in 1837 the slabs of granite needed for construction were ever ferried out to the shoal or how those intrepid builders managed to raise such an edifice on that narrow spit of land. But there it was with "Keeper's Quarters Provided," as the Coast Guard manual indicated. This was the home that Mr. Ray offered Adela.

In the summer a ferry ran the twenty-four miles between Bridgeport and Port Jefferson, keeping far to the east of the dangerous shoal. In summer, too, you could watch the porpoises rolling and diving as they followed the track of food that the ferry passengers threw to them. There was a sturdy rowboat that the Keeper could use for moving around the shoal on his inspections and a motor launch for trips to shore for shopping. For the most part the water was warm and calm and it was fun to ride the fifteen miles bumping through the waves that never ran higher than a half-foot.

In the winter there was nothing. When the rain came it

came slant-wise straight for the windows. It seemed there was never a time when the wind wasn't high – too high to open a window or get a clear glimpse of the far shore. "Locked in," explained Mr. Ray to my father, "we were locked in until spring."

They weathered the first winter, Mr. Ray scrupulously caring for the beacon, climbing the high stairs with the wind like a torrent whipping the tower. Adela tried to keep busy, sewing curtains, knitting afghans in pretty colors to make their rooms more habitable, more "like home." But as their second winter approached she found nothing to occupy her. "Restless all the time," explained Mr. Ray. "Like a cat before a storm, just pacing and turning with no place to rest." And then the storm came. They got signals ahead of time and did what they could to secure their boats and protect their windows with plywood but nothing they could have done could have protected them against the storm that battered them in the week after Christmas. "A day and two nights altogether," Mr. Ray said. "After the first night Adela, she didn't say anything. I tried to hold her in my arms but she fought me." He stopped for a long pause. "When it stopped, the boats were gone. Some windows were broke but we were safe. I tried to tell her but she couldn't hear me. She hid beneath the table in the kitchen and I couldn't get her out."

My father cleared his throat but he didn't say anything. I was standing by the window and when I looked down I saw that the rock I was holding was soaking wet, that my hands were soaking wet. I put the rock down, trying not to make a sound, and I rubbed my hands to dry them against my skirt. Fear had worked its way from my heart into my hands. It was my first experience – but not my last – of elemental terror, a fear so profound that no reasoning can exorcise it. I can still conjure up the image of Adela, whom I never saw, crouching and mute, inside her prison.

I don't know if Mr. Ray told us more that day. I think it was only later that I learned that when the Coast Guard came to rescue them he carried Adela to the boat and brought her to shore. She wanted to go home and he drove her back to her family in South Fork. They never lived together again. "She just wasn't able," he explained. He stayed on at Middle Ground for a couple of years and then was offered the post at Old Field Light.

"He's lonely," my father would say as we'd walk across the park and knock at the lighthouse door. Mr. Ray never spoke much to me but he was always kind, giving me a special rock from his collection or taking out a book with pictures of lighthouses for me to pore through. One winter day we had stayed longer than usual and Mr. Ray looking at his watch said it was time for him to "light the light." My father was helping me with my coat when Mr. Ray smiled at me and said, "Would you like to come up?" Would I? I didn't know and I looked toward my father. "Of course she'd like to go," my father said, pushing me toward the stairs. With Mr. Ray leading the way and my father following we climbed another set of stairs. At the top was a heavy door which opened onto a flight of narrow circular stairs which seemed to have no end. "You got to be careful here," warned Mr. Ray. "We're fine," said my father, "we're fine, aren't we?" But I didn't answer. I wasn't at all sure if I was fine. When I looked down, my stomach turned over because I could see straight down all the way we had come. Step by careful step we made it to the top and then I knew that it was all worth the death-defying climb.

## ENCOUNTERS

We were high, high above all that I thought of as the world. Beneath us was spread out the geometric pattern of the park and then beyond – the blue, blue waters of the Sound. The sun, still above the horizon, lit the waves into fire points. There was water wherever I looked, almost blinding in the sun's rays. For the first time in my young life I had an intuition of eternity. I didn't want to move, I didn't want to speak. I wanted it to last forever. But even as I watched, the light changed. The sun was sinking. The moment of eternity was gone.

This is where fantasy tangles with memory and overtops it. Reason tells me that "lighting the light" must have meant reaching out and pushing a switch; we were after all living in the century of electricity. But that is not what I remember. I remember a girl standing stiffly by the huge globe reaching out to take a lighted taper from the lighthouse keeper. Then guided by his hand she holds it over the wick until it bursts into flame. The sun was still too bright for the light to illumine the waters but for the girl it didn't matter. She knew. She knew she had illumined the world. She had saved ships from foundering. She had saved sailors from a watery grave.

For some reason I must need that image because even now it is pure and clean in my imagination. Light switches will not do. I need a lighted taper. I need to see the fire and feel its warmth as it flares up. I need to know that it is that human gesture which lights the world.

I think I remember that Mr. Ray let me light the light a couple of other times but it is the first time that shapes my image. Not long after, Old Field Light was automated and Mr. Ray moved away. In the evenings you could still visit the park and watch while the strong electric beam flashed red, then green, across the waters. In time the Coast Guard decided that even this beacon was unnecessary and the light was disconnected. Middle Ground Light (or Stratford Shoal as it is officially called) is still operative. It, too, was automated but the two-story Gothic structure with its Keeper's Quarters remains. If you check the "Inventory of Historic Light Stations," however, you will find an added note: Not Open to the Public.

ENCOUNTERS

# MAZDA AND JANE

Miss Jane Lindsey (she was always "Miss Lindsey" even to the other servants) was Nanny/Governess for the youngest of the Lloyds' three daughters. Eluned was probably about seven the summer we played together. Unlike most of the families in our residential community on Long Island's North Shore, the Lloyds came only for the summer, bringing with them their retinue of servants. It was a self-contained household. Perhaps this was why they never quite fit in. Mr. Lloyd traveled to New York daily and Mrs. Lloyd, it was said, was forced to keep to her room most of the time, suffering from a "lingering illness." Gwendolyn and Gwyneth, the older girls, managed well enough with a group of local teen-agers but Eluned was a lonely child held in tutelage to her Nanny. There was nothing spontaneous in Eluned's days. Her life was simply a series of responses to Miss Lindsey's direction. In reply to my complaint that she wasn't any fun to be with, my mother gave no quarter. "Be nice to Eluned" became my mother's summer theme.

Thus I became – if not her friend, at least a companion. Seven years old is probably too young for friendship but we managed to get along, playing the few games Miss Lindsey

## MAZDA AND JANE

found acceptable and spending the long warm afternoons on the Lloyds' private beach. Miss Lindsey never wore beach clothes. She wore the same long skirt – always a dark color – and a starchy blouse. Her black hair was combed back with a discreet bun at her neck. She followed us down the steep track which the servants used, a little east of the well-manicured path reserved for the family adults. Behind her followed Mazda, the Lloyds' chauffeur, wheeling a little truck with all the paraphernalia we would need during the afternoon. Mazda was stocky, dark-complexioned – and silent. And why not? No one spoke to him beyond giving him directions which needed no reply. We were, I suppose, too young to question the propriety of a grown man being subject to the peremptory demands of two children. He carried our dolls to the car, carefully packing in the diminutive steamer trunks full of dolls' clothes. He moved the seats and arranged the pillows for our comfort while Eluned and I sat in lavish splendor in the meticulously polished Rolls Royce.

What Mazda did when he was not at our service we never knew except that he lived alone in a little stone gatehouse just off the main drive to the Lloyd estate. It was my father (who had a facility for listening to everyone) who explained that Mazda had come to America from Hungary with his wife but she ("poor soul") had been unable to adjust to this lonely life for which nothing had prepared her. Her actions had become strange and frightening and Mazda, in order to keep his job, had been forced to put her in an institution.

But if we commanded Mazda we were counter-checked by Miss Lindsey. There was not a moment of Eluned's day that was not regimented (nor mine when I was with her). Our lunch of a broiled lamb chop, a baked potato, a green vegetable and a detestable desert called Junket (it was either yellow or lavender) never varied. Nor did the nap that followed. Only once a month, on a Thursday afternoon, did our regime change. That was the day we had an "Outing." The car was prepared and driven up to the portico in front of the main entrance. Mazda stood at attention – but he was not in his uniform. He wore a jacket and tie of some dark color – like a business man. Jane Lindsey, too, seemed to be what the housemaid called in disdain "gussied up." This meant mostly that she wore a hat and carried gloves. Miss Lindsey sat in the front seat with Mazda. Eluned and I, also somewhat gussied up in print dresses and white Maryjanes, sat in the back, trying to look, as Miss Lindsey put it, Ladylike. We were "going to lunch." The formality of the occasion seemed to demand silence and none of us spoke until we stopped in front of one of the small modest Tea Shoppes which dotted that section of Long Island's north shore.

We were given a glass of water and a menu which we studied – although there was no need. Miss Lindsey ordered for us and the menu rarely varied: sliced chicken on white bread with a small lettuce salad. It was the dessert, however, which made the day. We could choose! A brownie topped with vanilla ice cream, a fruit pie (in season) topped with vanilla ice cream or strawberry shortcake topped with whipped cream. Lunch always took a long time. Mazda sat next to Miss Lindsey. I don't remember what he ordered but I don't think it was chicken sandwiches. Sometimes he would leave ahead of us to see something about the car. But the Thursday I remember he stayed with us. Miss Lindsey paid the bill and then gathered us in front of her. We were, she explained, going to have a special treat. We were going to the movies. If Miss Lindsey expected giggles of joy she was disappointed. The news – we were going to the movies – so beyond our anticipation – left us numb. "Come along," she said and pushed us toward the car where Mazda was holding the door open for us.

As we drove along, Miss Lindsey turned to us and explained that this was going to be our secret, that it was just for the four of us, our special secret which we would never tell even to our parents. Nothing is more delicious for a seven-year old than a secret and Eluned and I closed our eyes, held hands and promised never, never to mention it. I had been to the movies with my father who loved the slapstick humor of Laurel and Hardy. For Eluned, however, this was surely a first. The Lloyds belonged to a religion which outlawed not only drinking and smoking, but card games, dancing and anything else that might be fun. Movies would clearly be unacceptable to Eluned's parents. I have often wondered how Jane and Mazda had dared to take us, dared to trust us. They were surely aware of how unacceptable their actions would seem to the Lloyds. Only desperation could explain it. The need to escape for even an hour into a world beyond their drab universe had made them reckless.

The movie theater was half empty when we arrived and Miss Lindsey chose our seats – halfway back and in the center. She pushed us in first and then sat with Mazda at her right. I don't know the name of the film – or indeed much else about it. This was the days of silent films and although I craned forward to read the explanatory titles they came at me too fast for my limited ability. I finally gave up, concentrating on the images and the musical background. I watched the beautiful young heroine; I watched the handsome young hero as they fell in love. I saw the dark bearded man who seemed always to be lurking in the background. I could feel Eluned getting shivery beside me. Then the elegant ball was over and the lights dimmed. The beautiful heroine lay alone on her bed, dreaming thoughts of love. Suddenly the French window began to slip open, the long lace curtains trembled in the breeze and standing there was . . . What? Was it the dark bearded man? Was it a ghost? . . . An evil spirit? . . . The devil himself? He stood there, unmoving, with the curtains fluttering behind him – and I screamed. I know I screamed because I felt Miss Lindsey's strong hand on my arm and heard her sibilant "Shshshsh!"

My heart pounded and I could not catch my breath. I could feel my chocolate brownie rise up in my throat but somehow I put my hand over my mouth and nothing bad happened. For the rest of the movie I closed my eyes and prayed not to be sick. Later when Mazda helped us into the car I was able to smile and thank Miss Lindsey for "our wonderful secret." That night I was faithful to my promise. I told my mother about lunch and about walking around in the park but I never mentioned the movie.

But my silence did nothing to allay my terror. I washed my face and brushed my teeth; I knelt and said my prayers, all the time dreading the moment when I would be left alone. When my mother bent over to kiss me goodnight I wanted more than anything for her to lie down next to me and keep me safe. Instead she turned off the light and asked, "Do you want the window open a little more; it's very warm tonight?" But I didn't want the window open, I didn't want a breeze to ruffle the curtains. I wanted to be safe from the terror that lurked just within my imagination. That night was the first of months of nightly terrors.

Two weeks later it was time for the Lloyds to return to New York for the winter and for me to return to school. But it was a different child who took her place in the second grade. The quiet, confident little girl of the first grade had undergone a sea change. The power of imagination had claimed her. Those images of terror were stronger than the routine of her daily life.

This was in the days before the sophistication of psychological counseling. Of course my mother talked it over with my teachers. Everyone was very kind but no one could ferret out the cause of my terror. "Did something happen?" was the reiterated question. Did something happen at school, on the way home from school? Did you meet someone? Did a strange man speak to you? When you have the scary dream what do you see?" After a while I could hardly tell them. The vision had blurred. I hardly saw anything. I was left simply with an intangible terror.

It was, of course, the promise of secrecy that kept the terror alive. I had never before experienced anything that had kept me from my mother's arms. Comfort had embraced me and dissipated all my fears. For the first time I was left alone. Every night when I woke up gasping or crying she came to my side, holding me, whispering assurances. But no assurance reached me. The chasm of silence barred me from her comfort. To all her questions, her efforts to reach my fears, I could only shake my head and keep my silence.

Looking back I am amazed at the strength of my promise. I had only to break my word to Miss Lindsey for my nightmare to be dissipated – or at least diminished. Simply to explain that we had gone to the movies and I had been terrified by the images would be enough. But I had promised not to tell. What kept me faithful to my word – at such cost? What did I think would happen if I told? That my mother would explain to my teacher and that my teacher would call Mrs. Lloyd? And then? Would Miss Lindsey lose her job because she shouldn't have taken us to the movies? And what would happen to her? And Mazda, too, lonely, silent Mazda. Would they have to go off together? Mazda in his uniform and Miss Lindsey in her silly little black hat. But where? In fact none of my fears were actualized. The following summer I continued to play dolls with Eluned and eat the lunches Miss Lindsey set before us. Mazda continued to carry our paraphernalia and polish his car. The clandestine movie was never mentioned.

Memories are often delusive. Perhaps I am imposing adult concerns on an eight-year-old imagination. But there was something that held me steady and kept me faithful to my promise. Looking back I see it as my first adult action, the first time I moved beyond the comfort and security of my family. Miss Lindsey and Mazda were no longer confined by their roles as governess and chauffeur; they had become two people to whom I had made a promise and in so doing had become responsible for them. I was in some strange way their caretaker. They had led me beyond my childhood world. They had asked something of me and I had promised. I hadn't known at the time what it would cost but in my childish inchoate way I knew I had to keep faith.

I never told my mother even after the Lloyds sold Penwith and moved back to New York permanently. Some time later we heard that Mrs. Lloyd had died of her "lingering illness" and that Mr. Lloyd had remarried. A decade later I saw a newspaper photo of Eluned, tawny-haired and sophisticated,

# MAZDA AND JANE

at a New York ball. Of Mazda and Miss Jane Lindsey we heard nothing.

# THE WRITING LIFE I

I think I was about ten when I read *Little Women* for the first time. I remember sitting up in bed one night with the book open on my lap. My mother was sitting on the side of the bed facing me. I don't know why she was there. Perhaps I was recovering from a cold. Perhaps it was evening and she had come in to say "Good night" and warn me to put the book away and turn off the light. Looking back I think it was the intimacy of the scene which made me so expansive. I was not a talkative child and most of my fears and longings were kept well concealed. But this time my dream tumbled out: I wanted to be a writer! My expectation was so passionate that I could not contain it. I wanted to write short stories like Jo, I explained. But before I could go on, my mother laughed. "Too much *Little Women*," she said, closing the book and reaching for the light switch.

It had not been meant as a rebuff. It was simply an adult's careless response to a child's babbling but unwittingly it had pierced my dream. I don't know what happened next. Did I bury my face in my pillow and cry? Did I go on talking, trying to show her how serious I was? I don't remember but I know that this must have been a pivotal moment because

I can conjure it up now, so many years later, with the same emotional force as when it happened. A less controlled child might have screamed that adolescent response to frustration: "I hate you, I hate you, I hate you." I know I did no such thing but I know I was burning with anger and resentment. And I know now that a seed had been planted – a seed I would not understand until much later, warning me that being a writer was not an easily accepted vocation.

It would make a more dramatic story if I could recount that from that night forward I clutched my dream secretly to my heart, yearning for the day when I would cloister myself in a book-laden room filling pages with deathless prose. But like most ten-year-olds, I found life too full and too demanding to find time to brood over my resentment. For the moment, school was enough to satisfy my aspirations. I attended a small private school which followed an experimental program replacing the established curriculum by a system of projects. Once the student had chosen her project she was guided and encouraged by a mentor who remained her single teacher for the semester.

It was a process demanding discipline and perseverance and for me it worked like a charm. In a sense I was an easy child to deal with. I wanted to write stories and I was willing to do whatever that goal demanded. I was so focused that I needed little more than occasional encouragement. My mentor directed me to read widely, to explore other countries and other cultures so that the characters in my stories would have substance and depth. I loved this work, I loved the demands on my imagination, I loved ferreting out the words which were just right for what I was trying to communicate. I was guided and encouraged but never controlled.

# ENCOUNTERS

In many ways it was a healthy approach to education, although looking back I realize that it short-changed me in many practical ways. I learned a great deal but in such a scattered way that when it came time to register for a good high school I was found to be seriously deficient in such subjects as science and math – all areas outside the parameters of my interest. My parents were justifiably anxious but their anxiety did not concern me. I was confident that I was good at the one thing I wanted to do: I could write. I had prizes to prove it.

But that was before I went off to a well-ordered Catholic boarding school and met Sister Paracleta. She was old – all nuns were old but Paracleta was older than most. She was slight of build and what I could see of her face was small-featured with narrow lips and a small straight nose. She had a low, expressionless voice which could wither even a Shakespeare soliloquy. Later I learned that she wrote poetry and looking back I wonder how much she must have suffered in the stifling atmosphere of teaching English to generations of adolescents.

But in my day it was not poetry which engaged Sister Paracleta but grammar, a subject as foreign to me as calculus. I had never been taught rules. I wrote by a kind of instinct formed by reading and listening. That all those lovely words which rose up spontaneously when I needed them had names and definitions bewildered me. To write five sentences, each using a participial phrase – Sister Paracleta's assignment – was beyond me. The explanations she gave us, the diagrams she put on the board to help us provided no help. I wrote five sentences hoping beyond hope that somehow a participial phrase might find its way in. It never did. I rewrote the sentences, as she demanded, but with no more success.

Finally I was assigned to come to her office every Tuesday evening where I would rewrite our assignment. Nothing worked and Tuesday evenings became my nightmare – and my solace! Although I hated the humiliation of being singled out for "extra help" I could accept even this for the joy of being in her office. Her office gave me back my life. For one hour a week I was swept away from the drab, colorless environment of boarding school and ushered into a world that my imagination craved. Her office was wonderful. The shelves were full of books and the walls covered with prints. Some were swirls of color almost dizzying in their intensity but what drew me most were the posters – exotic posters of far-away cities: London, Rome, Venice, Barcelona. I sat there comforted by the glorious landscapes and the freedom they offered while Sister Paracleta buried herself in correcting papers. After a while she would look up, "Have you finished?" she would ask. But I had finished nothing. At the end she would sigh and take my paper. It was clear to her that the evening had been a failure, but for me it had renewed my spirit and left me with a memory of life.

It was inevitable that this would become a battle of wills. I continued to write as I had always written, ignoring her directions. I soon became "That impossible child." It was bad karma for both of us that Sister Paracleta remained my English teacher for my four years of high school.

What seems extraordinary to me is that even in those lackluster years I never lost my dream of being a writer. Since my English class provided no access, I scribbled on the side, shaving time from other assignments, even using a precious half-hour of "free time" when we could listen to records, gossip in the "rec room," take forbidden walks in the garden between the convent and the school. By the time I arrived at college I had given up on English teachers but not on writing.

My good karma is that college gave me back everything that high school had taken away. Within the first month I erased my initial decision to be a math major – a decision born less out of interest in math than out of a cynical judgment that math was not subject to a teacher's whims. By second semester I had embarked on an English major, filling my curriculum with literature. I read with undisciplined passion, the passion of coming upon everything for the first time. I found Yeats and Donne and Hopkins. But more than everything else I found Greek drama. I had signed up for a course in Greek Literature in Translation which turned out to be taught by one of the worst teachers I ever had. But, no matter, I discovered Sophocles and was so dazed that I skipped all my classes for two days while I was swept into a tidal wave of Greek drama.

And, of course, I wrote. I went from short stories to poetry. I lived in a world of image and metaphor. I wanted to be wonderful. I wanted to be a writer who would leave my readers in awe. I wanted my writing – and even my speech – to be so fresh that, as Hemingway advised, it would seem that my words were being used as though they had never been used before. The fact that I flunked botany, was debarred from German for over-cutting and had three room-mates in a single year didn't dampen my spirit.

By the end of my sophomore year I had shaken myself free from the adolescent cynicism high school had bred in me. I liked my Catholic college, I liked my Catholic friends. Somewhere along those years came an unanticipated revelation. I discovered God, God not as an academic subject but as an experienced reality. It was not a thunderbolt-revelation, it was a slow, unobtrusive presence. "As once at a crash Paul or as Austin with a lingering-out sweet skill" Hopkins had written. My epiphany was the lingering-out sweet skill kind. God was there; he was present to me. In time my epiphany began to take over my life. If what I experienced was true, I asked myself, then what should my response be?

The year following my graduation found me seriously considering the question of a "vocation," that word from the dictionary of the Catholic language which meant a celibate life in a religious congregation. My decision, to those I revealed it, was not greeted with enthusiasm. My mother saw it as the waste of a good mind and a not-unattractive body. My father for whom I was the beloved Benjamin was overwhelmed with Irish melancholy at the thought of losing me. The Ursuline sisters to whom I was offering this precious gift seemed uncertain that they would accept it. My resume, it was pointed out, did not speak of the steady pursuit of virtue. I couldn't have agreed more; virtue had little attraction for me. It was God who attracted me – that Great Indefinable Metaphor who surely would not limit me to a life of mere virtue.

Ultimately I received a grudging assent from religious authorities and, "leaving the world," I entered the Ursuline novitiate in Beacon, New York. What had happened to my passion to be a great writer? To this day I hardly know. I do know that I saw no dramatic conflict. Unlike Gerard Manley Hopkins I did not destroy my "writings" before I left for the novitiate. Such a step predicated a maturity I had not reached.

Hopkins understood that the life of the writer and the life of the consecrated person were not easily combined. It was years before I faced that radical conflict.

For the next seven years the passion to write lay dormant. Life was simply too full to give room to anything else. There is an old Dutch expression, "full as an egg," to describe a situation bursting at the seams. My life was in those first years "full as an egg." Life "inside" had a rhythm and a protocol which encompassed everything. The arcane rituals of religious life demanded constant attention. And then, in addition to the daily minutiae, there were the overarching reaches of our developing spirituality. The trick was to keep everything in place. Clearly there was no time (or space) for the imaginative excursions of the writer's life.

Nor did I miss them. Perhaps if I had I would have left. Only once in those years did I face the possibility of "returning to the world." It was a bright October day and I was hanging towels on the clothesline behind the novitiate building. I was reaching up when suddenly the golden mountains and the fantasy clouds scudding through that blue sky almost undid me. I wanted to be free; I wanted to lose myself in something beautiful – something here and now. The mystery of eternal life and eternal love seemed for a moment very drab and lifeless compared to the October breeze that blew through my veil. But the bell rang and I hung up the last towel and took my basket indoors. The moment never came again.

It was not until the year following my perpetual profession that the question of writing arose. During my interview with our provincial she asked me to write a "pamphlet" –

something short and readable about the first Ursulines to come to North America in 1639. I knew little about this history, nothing about what such a project would entail but it didn't matter. I went to chapel with my heart pounding. Was this how the Widow of Naim felt when Jesus – beyond all expectation – gave her back her son?

But being given back a life that one had accepted as dead was, I soon discovered, a complex blessing. The "pamphlet" which originally I had expected to put together during a summer soon stretched into the academic year. The provincial who had initiated this work was replaced by another with little interest beyond the immediate duties of the classroom and the community. My plea for a little extra time was heard with a cold ear. The warning – first delivered before my entrance into the novitiate – was issued again, this time in more concrete form: I must be careful, lest I become "singular" (another word from the Catholic dictionary) and find myself outside the protective routines of community life.

Looking back I see that I was close to a crisis but at the time the situation seemed manageable. I had no desire to leave religious life but neither was I willing to sacrifice my writing. Although I was already burdened to my limit with four college courses to teach and a variety of extracurricular activities, I was determined to work things out so that I could do both. And thus began a life in which everything – teaching, recreation, community service – was cut to the bone in order to create the free time I needed. In my favor, I must say that I was scrupulously careful in my duties. My classes were always well-prepared, I remained generous in community activities but always pulsing in the back of my mind like a heartbeat was that "object of my affection" which conditioned my life.

The work had soon passed beyond the boundaries of a pamphlet. I had begun to write a book. I had learned early on that pleading for extra time was not only useless but created a suspect atmosphere. I kept my silence and continued to work. Thirteen years after I had received the initial request, I had a completed book-size manuscript. And then what? In my superb innocence I put it in a discarded typing paper box, wrapped it in brown paper and sent it to Doubleday – the only publisher I knew who had a Catholic Books Department. I know now that such unsolicited manuscripts are referred to as "slush" and more often than not do not even get a reading. But innocence is a wonderful protector and I waited not expectantly but at least with hope. In less than a month I received a letter saying that there was interest in my manuscript and asking if I would "come in" and chat about a contract.

Joy knocked me off my feet and I took to my bed with the worst headache I had ever had. What now? I had told almost no one – least of all my superior – that the pages I had been dickering with for years had gone off to a publisher and that it now seemed headed for publication. When I finally "confessed" she made no protest although the frown lines that pulled her eyebrows together were sufficient indication of a certain apprehension. She neither congratulated me nor reprimanded me. She simply nodded, gave me money for a ticket on the New Haven Railroad to take me to New York City, assigned me a companion (we never traveled alone), and wished me well. Within the next two weeks I signed a contract and began revisions on a six hundred page manuscript.

# THE WRITING LIFE I

Just fourteen years from the starting gate my book was published.

ENCOUNTERS

# **FINDING MY VOICE**

The admonition I remember most from my childhood is SPEAK UP! My mother used it when she waited for me to answer her question. My father used it (in exasperation) when he was showing off his youngest (and unresponsive) offspring to a friend. The man in the ice cream store said it as he bent over the counter trying to understand my mumbled desires. My first grade teacher (Miss Pennwarden) tried it for a while but then gave up when her coaxing had no results. My Aunt Loretta had a different take: "What's the matter? Did the cat get your tongue?" she asked, giving me a poke with her elbow. We had a cat but he seemed as silent as I so her question made no sense to me.

Many years later when I was taking a course in psychology I read that abused or abandoned children often suffer speech loss. But I grew up at the very antipodes of abandoned. Although my mother, recently married at the age of forty-two, found me a surprise, certainly I was not unwanted. She set to work with the single-minded industry which had ruled her life to prepare herself for the unanticipated role of motherhood. She approached life cerebrally so it is no surprise that she set about amassing a library to help her in her new task. One set of books I still recall. They were a set of ten (or twelve?) volumes, bound in black leather with red backing and gold titles. The one I remember most began, "When your child asks a question." Every few pages there were whole page illustrations of a mother (beautifully dressed and coiffed) bending over a child gazing at its parent with eager anticipation. The hitch for my mother was that I never asked a question. Perhaps had there been some opportunity for horizontal conversation at home I might have been forced into speaking. But as the only child of older parents, all conversation was vertical. I began early to listen and observe. It was the way to learn and for me much more interesting than talking. All my needs were always taken care of almost before I was aware of them. So what was to be gained by talking?

My mother who expected things to go according to the book became increasingly anxious at my silence. My father, who had parented several children in a former marriage, was more cavalier. He shrugged. "She'll talk when she goes to school," he assured her. Alas, he was wrong. The available public school was several miles away. There was no bus service in those days and my father drove me both ways. I carried my lunch with me in a bright tin box: a sandwich, some cut-up carrots and celery, a thermos of milk, and cookies. I hated the whole thing. I hated eating out of a tin box and I hated it more because my lunch neither looked nor smelled like anybody else's lunch.

Until the end of my fifth year we had lived in a big brownstone house in Brooklyn. Down the street and around the corner from us was the butcher store with sawdust on the floor and a bulging grey and white cat who slept at the end of the counter. Next to the butcher was the milk and cheese shop where we sometimes went to buy extra milk when my mother couldn't wait until the next morning for the milk man's delivery. Two blocks away and one street over was the elementary school with its gray stone arch and formidable entrance.

On weekends my father always took me for a walk. After we had sat and fed the "chippies" in Prospect Park we came home the way that would take us past the school. That was going to be "my school" my father always explained. With little education himself he had a passion to see that I had it all. On the first day of school, he would tell me, holding my hand as we looked up at the school's high windows, he would bring me himself and the principal would see how smart I was and put me in the first grade right away without any test. But just when I was old enough to start school we moved to Long Island and I lost the butcher with his purring cat, the chippies in the park and – "my" school.

My new school was an alien world. My classmates came mostly from neighboring farms. Their fathers grew acres of potatoes and cauliflower. Being a city kid I had never seen a cauliflower outside its rightful place in the grocery store. The kids all seemed to know each other and they all had unpronounceable names: Jonaitis and Lesousky are the two I remember. Perhaps I might have been coaxed into speech had I been surrounded by O'Reillys and Sullivans and if the girl with whom I shared a two-seat desk was not called Miyada. But I found nothing here to tempt me out of my comfortable burrow of silence.

School, however, put an end to my mother's fear that she

had brought a retarded child into the world. School proved that I was bright. No flash card daunted me. I could read. I could read silently and I could read aloud, clearly and with expression. I passed first grade with flying colors but every report card carried the same ominous observation: She finds difficulty in expressing herself. They could not have been more wrong. It was not that I found speech difficult; it simply didn't interest me. I must have been a pragmatist at an early stage. Speech seemed to me to require a lot of effort for very little return. The world, as I perceived it, seemed quite complete without any interference from me. And I, too, was quite complete. I don't think I was lazy. It was simply that I preferred to conserve my energy for what seemed to me important.

At the end of my first year of school I was felled by an extreme attack of whooping cough and was warned by the doctor to stay quiet in order to keep the coughing down. Far from being a restriction this became an unexpected opportunity for it gave me time to explore a magic world. The magic of reading I had already discovered but now I was finding the flip side of reading: the magic of writing. I began to realize that those printed words which were claiming my attention more and more did not just appear by magic, they were put there by someone. There was a prior act: the act of writing. Just as you could learn to read, maybe you could learn to write.

"Writing" as we had practiced it in school had bored me: copying over words from the blackboard, forming the letters just so, keeping them on the line, letting the tails hang down but not too far. But that was not writing, not real writing. Real writing was far more exciting and demanding. All the stuff they told you to do in school was just copying, just writing over what someone else had already written. Writing was something else, mysterious and wonderful. For me it was the very reverse of speech. Writing was putting on paper the secret thoughts you guarded in silence. With writing you could take your time. You could cross out and correct. But the wonder was that you could keep all this secret. In this writing world there was no one standing next to you saying, "Speak up!"

That whooping-cough summer give me my lifetime passport to the universe. By the time September came I had written my first poem, "To a Dahlia" and my first short story, "In the Farmhouse." The "Dahlia" has happily disappeared but I still have the first two pages of "In the Farmhouse." It's distinguished by its correct spelling, by the inkblots in the margin and by its boring unoriginality. But even so there was a sign of something that someday would enhance my writing career. I was alert to the atmosphere around me. I had never been in a farmhouse but I had listened to the whispered conversations as my class was herded into the basement cafeteria for lunch. I heard Miyada telling Ursula how her sister had forgotten to turn the oven off so the bread (dark thick bread that she brought to school daily) was burned and her mother whipped the backs of her legs. I heard how the kittens were born in the barn and how Jason's older brother took them and drowned them in the pond because they had too many. I heard how you could get hurt on the big farm machines if you weren't careful and how they bought clothes and shoes through the thick catalogs – like New York telephone directories – they sometimes brought to school.

I thought about the burned bread and wondered if it

was so burned they had to throw it out. I closed my eyes and wondered how it felt to get the backs of your legs whipped. What did her mother use? Was it just her hands or did she have something harder.? And did Letizia cry or was she just quiet? Thinking about the kittens was even worse. I didn't know much about kittens. I only knew about the butcher's cat and it was hard to believe she had ever been a baby kitten. The story of the kittens was so mysterious that I spent nights keeping sleep away by trying to imagine what had happened. To kill something. How could that be? To take these tiny things and do what? Drown. I knew that if you were drowned you were dead but how would you do that to little baby kittens? I thought of asking my mother about it but decided against it. I couldn't tell her about the kittens. It was too terrible to talk about. And I thought about the boy who had to take these little things to the pond. Did he beg his father not to make him do? Did he have to watch while the kittens died? And his father. The father who told him to do this thing. Even at night with my eyes closed I could not imagine such a person. It was like the cruel man Blue Beard I had read about in our fairy tale book.

It was all part of the secret world which could keep me occupied for hours. But when I came in from school and sat at the bright clean kitchen table drinking my cocoa I had nothing to say to my mother's daily question: "What happened in school today?" I didn't really lie when I said, "Nothing." Nothing really had happened. I had listened to what had already happened, I listened to other people's lives and began to make them my own.

Of course, "In the Farmhouse" revealed nothing of this. It was a little story of a brother and sister who lived on a farm and helped in the kitchen and like me had kind parents who loved them. Anything more would have to wait. But I had begun. I had begun to develop that basic requirement for writing: I was, unconsciously of course, developing my memory. Many years later when I read that Ernest Hemingway, suffering a debilitating depression, had refused shock treatments because he feared they would destroy his memory, I understood his decision. Without his memory, he declared, he would not be a writer.

It was inevitable that I would go to college and major in English, spending most of my time writing highly immature short stories for a class in creative writing. Perhaps it was inevitable, too, that I would enter the convent and become a professor of English literature. My childhood dream of a quiet house by the water where I would be a "true writer" slipped away, lost for a while in the clutter of academia. It was years before I recovered my dream but when I did I discovered my voice at last.

Although during that time I had written several biographies, I was close to retirement when I wrote my first fiction. *Seven Sons* was a mystery story, pure and simple. It had no pretensions of anything else. I used a pseudonym, fearful of the scorn of my academic colleagues that "one of theirs" had stooped so low. *Seven Sons* sold in drug stores and airport lounges. I got royalty checks – but that was not the point. The point – the wonderful exhilarating point – was that I found I could write dialog. I had found my voice in the voices of others.

All those years of remembering provided me with a wonderful gift. I not only saw the kitchen of the farmhouse and saw the pond where the kittens were drowned; I heard the voices of the people, the extraordinary distinct unique voice quality of each one. Later I would be called a "visual writer" and it was true: I could get the scene right, paint the picture in all its detail. But there was something more. I could get voices right. For years I had been listening not only to what was being said around me but to the expression, the tone, the timbre of the voice. And I remembered it all; it played in my head with the fullness of recalled music.

With the confidence I felt from *Seven Sons* I embarked on a more serious endeavor: a novel about nuns. Vatican II with its unanticipated consequences had put nuns on the front page. What had happened to the Good Sisters? Where had they gone? They were no longer seen in their distinguished garb; they were no longer visible in that bulwark of Catholic life – the parochial school. Convents were only half-occupied, in some cases being sold entirely. What, indeed, had happened to the Good Sisters? There were any number of essays by the nuns themselves and by others explaining how they were working out the changes recommended by Vatican II. There were sociological statistics. There were studies in the "new psychology" of self-fulfillment. I was inundated by defenses and explanations but throughout it all I did not hear a single voice.

I needed to hear not a thesis but a voice. I needed to write a novel. *Accidental Grace* was the story of a group of nuns struggling to find a way in a new world. Hearing the distinguishing quality which would characterize the speech of each individual was, I soon discovered, a difficult task. In *Seven Sons* I had women and men, wealthy people, poor servants – their speech easily distinguished by their roles.

But nuns! Here I was faced with seventeen characters – all women, all mature, all teachers, all trained in the same religious mode and for the most part all from the same economic bracket.

Yet I knew from my own convent experience how different nuns' voices are even when they are saying the same thing. Writing *Accidental Grace* was a process of hearing beneath the surface to reach that distinctive coloring, that musical timbre that reveals far more than what is said. When it is done well, it reveals the character's identity. "Getting it right." Getting it right was how I identified the process of writing *Accidental Grace*. Most of the time I lost sight of the fact that I was writing a novel. I was simply "getting it right" – getting right the voices that would reveal seventeen women in their most profound realities. I spent hours "listening to voices" until I could hear the sharp bark of Clement's need for justification, Gregory's hesitant Irish lilt, Angela's wistful half-sentences, Edwarda's unremitting sibilants. At the end I had created a convent, a gathering of voices seeking a future.

I loved writing *Accidental Grace*. Partially, of course, because it was a good story, a cogent narrative explanation of what had happened to the Good Sisters. But far beyond that it had provided an answer to that childhood admonition: Speak Up. I had spoken up. I had found my voice. But my voice was manifold. My voice was the voice of all those others – the remembered and the imagined. I could still hear the recording of Jonas Lesousky and the drowned kittens or Miyada and her sister's burned bread. The timbre of their voices was still with me

*Accidental Grace* was indeed a gift for me. It gave me my

voice or – perhaps better – proved that I had been right all along: the small narrow radius of my individual voice was unimportant compared to the multiple voices playing inside me. But some things never change. The Miss Pennwardens of the world are still working on me. Although I am rarely asked to be on a committee these days, when in that dark moment I am asked my opinion, the same thing invariably happens. The chairperson pushes the microphone toward me and asks, "Would you mind speaking up?"

# ENCOUNTERS

## A WRITER'S DIARY

*"I am not a scholar. I am not in the least an intellectual which is not to say that when I hear the word "intellectual" I reach for my gun, but only to say that I do not think in abstracts. During the years when I was an undergraduate at Berkeley I tried with a kind of hopeless, late-adolescent energy, to buy some temporary visa into the world of ideas, to forge for myself a mind that could deal with the abstract.*

*In short I tried to think. I failed. My attention veered back to the specific, to the tangible, to what was generally considered by everyone I knew . . . the peripheral. I would try to contemplate the Hegelian dialectic and would find myself concentrating instead on a flowering pear tree outside my window."*

Joan Didion, "Why I Write," *NY Times Book Review*, 1976.

Sept. 20

Here I am at last: in my office, sitting before my computer, ready . . . ready, I guess, to start *Encounters*. I'm trying to remember the kind of ecstasy I felt last spring when this idea first came to me. I was in Montana, having finished the final rewrites (I thought!) of *Lady Blackrobes* and recognizing that

I would never do another book demanding that amount of research and travel. Age, health and especially the macular degeneration that had affected my left eye were serious disabilities. The weeks of reading microfilm for this last book had just about been my undoing. It was clear: Never again.

So had I come to the end of my writing career? Terrifying thought. I needed to write; it is who I am. And that was when the idea of *Encounters* rose up before me. Simple! No travel, no research, just a series of reflective essays on remembered events, people, places. It need not be complete or strictly biographical; it need not be chronological. It could be . . . whatever I wanted. "Piece a' cake," for sure.

Sept. 24

I'm really serious about keeping a diary – a "writer's" diary – which means that I want to keep it about writing or the things that touch my writing – health, other responsibilities, what moves me forward, what pushes me back. Years ago I read that Steinbeck (I think it was Steinbeck) kept a big ledger. On the right he wrote his novel (not sure which one) and on the left a diary about writing the novel. Seems like a fascinating idea. Maybe I can do something like that – a record of how a book gets written – how <u>this</u> book gets written.

Sept. 28

OK. So how will it get written? What am I going to write about? An open subject. It seems that I am heading toward a book of reflective essays. Maybe fifteen or twenty in all. But how to choose out of all possible subjects? They don't need to be chronological. I don't want them all on the same subject or from the same period of my life. What do I want? Some event or place or person that has moved me profoundly – not necessarily something of prime importance but something that makes my heart pound. I've always been fascinated by moments that stand out in my memory as vividly, as clearly as the moment they happened, even though they don't seem to be of special significance. What is it? That strange pull with power to plunge us back into the past. That's what I want: the powerfully remembered.

Oct. 1

My mother's birthday. Were she alive I think she would be pleased that I am writing – especially if it makes me famous!! I did some good work the other day. Now: to continue. I need lots of blank time, time to stare at the wall.

Oct. 15

Two weeks since my last entry. Part of it was doctors' appointments. The leg problem is getting dramatic. I can hardly stand at times, so much pain. Oh, well. On with the real stuff. Out of those empty days has come an interesting list of possible topics to explore. I'll list them here and talk about them later

- My Buddhist retreat in Taiwan and its aftermath
- My father, the great story teller who left me his genes
- From being a silent kid to being a dialog writer
- About writing *Solo Voices*
- Childhood memory of lighting the beacon on the Old Field Light
- Learning God – a whopper: Knowing God/Learning God. Big difference. Fascinating

- Mazda and Jane – strange childhood memory of a governess and a chauffeur
- Nova Nada Journal – my weeks seeking solitude in the wilds of Nova Scotia
- The stroke of lightning that hit me with macular degeneration
- Swatches from a Taiwan Diary – this will be fun, I think – and all ready for me
- The Buddhist nun – a powerful and mysterious memory from Taiwan
- Writing Life I – this is an effort to find out what it is all about
- Writing Life II – more of the same and deeper
- Walking to Cathay – decision to go to Taiwan
- Forgiveness – mostly, I think, about forgiving my mother or asking for forgiveness????
- Adolescent Depression – A bad siege of this when I was 12-14. No one paid attention
- Writer's Diary – I hope to keep a journal; maybe some of this may be culled. Interesting
- Brother Wolf – 15 years of correspondence with a Methodist Minister from Missouri
- Seeking Solitude – Bewildered and mostly negative response to Vatican II

This is what these days of thinking have produced. I am sure there will be more and sure, too, that some of these won't work out. Amazing what emerges from that great unmapped land of memory.

Oct. 17

Out of all those possible topics I chose as a beginning writing *Solo Voices* – my dearly beloved and still unpublished novel. I think I will call it "Homecoming."

Oct. 18

I suppose I thought it was logical to start with a piece about writing. As it turns out I am finding it very difficult. Maybe anything would be difficult. I'm out of the swing. And in addition this is such different stuff from all the historical matter I have been dealing with.

Oct. 19

I'm afraid to see what I have written. Within the last week I have been robbed of all faith in what I am doing. I have begun to doubt that I will ever do it, that instead my days will be taken up with little things, that I will not have the energy (either physical or psychological) to take on this book. And then, the even more basic question: for what? There may well be no audience. So is it enough to write just to write, to order all these random thoughts, to confront my memories and to dredge up more memories? What is it that Rilke says: If you can not be a poet then you should not be a poet. Can I not be a writer? I remember my shrink saying that it's not a question of how good you are; it's a question of the passion to create. At the moment I don't feel that passion but when I think of what life would be like if I weren't writing or at least not thinking about writing, it is too bleak to imagine.

Oct. 20

I did, finally, have the courage to read over what I had done of "Homecoming." Not as bad as I had thought but ... too wordy, too self-conscious, even a little precious as to vocabulary! Well, there you are: it is, as I have told generations of aspiring young writers, a question of paring down, cutting out, keeping your finger on the delete key! But here it is more than that. There is something nauseatingly self-conscious about what I have written. "Behold me: a writer at work!" Ugh.

Oct. 22

Maybe "Homecoming" is not quite as bad as I had thought. I gave up on the computer and took a yellow pad and began to jot down some notes. Hardly an outline but a series of jottings which perhaps will help me organize. Why am I finding this so difficult? I would give up but I think that if I can bring it off this could be a really good piece. The thing is that this kind of writing must be so . . . what? . . . just right because style is just about everything. So different from the kind of narration I am used to. Closer to poetry and very scary . . . but more satisfying, too.

Nov. 1

Oh where have all the flowers gone . . . .

Dec. 12

More doctors and tests. Hard to keep writing with so much pain. Never mind. Better than sitting at home. I decided to give myself a break and look through my Taiwan Diary to see if there was stuff I could use. I was really encouraged. So much of it seemed fresh and interesting. I checked over a number of entries, trying to keep a balance of funny, reflective, informative. Lots to choose from. I think it will be a good piece. And, ah, so effortless to put together!

Jan. 10

I suppose it was a natural to go from the Taiwan Diary to my experience at the Buddhist monastery. This was one of my favorite days in Taiwan. The monastery high up the mountain, the pure, silent Buddhist nun, the wiry little Austrian priest. And, of course, the Swiss chalet built in the midst of Chinese mountains. What is to be made of it all?

Jan. 14

I came across this sentence in an essay by Alfred Kazin:

> In a very real sense, the writer writes in order to teach himself, to understand himself, to satisfy himself; the publishing of his ideas, though it brings gratification, is a curious anticlimax.

And I would add: he writes to bring clarity to the chaos of human experience.

Jan. 15

I spent an infuriating hour reading two weeks of the *NY Times Book Review*. So many boring books but worse than boring are the lists of the same people writing the same thing and continuing to make the top of the Best Seller List. Then out of my memory came this cheery sentence: "A best-seller is the gilded tomb of a mediocre talent." Ah Bravo! Logan Pearsall Smith, if my memory serves me.

Jan. 18

I have put "Homecoming" aside for now – maybe forever. I couldn't pull myself out of the pit. What I was doing wasn't writing; it was some sort of pseudo-psychology. I suppose it can always be a temptation to write yourself out in order to sharpen your identity but that isn't what I want to do. I want memory to be cleaner than that. Having written that, I'm not quite sure what I mean but I know that there is something – not something that I must find but something that will find me. But for now "Homecoming" is postponed.

Jan. 24

Today the *NY Times* announced the death of Mireille Marokvia, a lady I had never heard of but whose obituary has cheered me mightily. She died in New Mexico at the age of ninety-nine. She had written two memoirs: one of her childhood in France and the second of her years in war-torn Germany. But what cheered me was the fact that she was, in her nineties, still writing – nothing major – sketches of her childhood, simple remembered events.

So, Mireille dear, stay with me, sustain me, keep me going.

Jan. 26

I haven't said much about the absent days – of which there have been many. Sometimes it was just a question of bad weather but mostly it was doctors and X-Rays and MRI's. I think I am getting closer to making a decision about surgery. I most surely have tried everything else. I have just finished a couple of weeks of "spinal decompression" which was supposed to give me speedy relief. Not so, not so. So this morning I said goodbye to the nice young man with his magic machine. I think he was glad to see me go.

# ENCOUNTERS

Jan. 30

Quite by accident I came across a book of essays by André duBus. I had read a lot of his short stories and loved them but I didn't know about the essays. I'm so glad I found them because there I found this terrific paragraph that only a writer could write:

> What is demanding and fulfilling is writing a single word, trying to write *le mot juste*, as Flaubert said; writing several of them, which become a sentence. When a writer does that, day after day, working alone with little encouragement, often with discouragement flowing in the writer's own blood and with an occasional rush of excitement that empties oneself, so that the self is for minutes longer in harmony with eternal astonishments and visions of truth, right there on the page on the desk, and when a writer does this work steadily enough to complete a ms long enough to be a book, the treasure is on the desk.

Mar. 3

Easy to see how unfaithful I have been. Actually I have been doing some writing even if I never got to keeping a diary. Too hard to think about what's happening. So little energy, so hard to keep going, so bewildering to figure out what exactly I am doing. Ice and snow doesn't help – my bones freeze up and my imagination hibernates. Maybe I am just a bear in a cave. But bears do produce cubs at the end of their hibernation. So cheer up! Maybe you will have something to show in the spring.

Apr. 6

My friend Irene's birthday and the day was a great present. I started "The Writing Life" and found myself flying. I was comfortable, engaged, confident. I knew my fingers were on the right keys. How does this happen? Is there anything more mysterious than this writing business? When you feel you have things in place you can end up being totally stymied. And then without warning the words come, *"le mot juste"* simply leaps out from its hiding place . . . and we smile at each other. Doing this piece is wonderfully affirming. When people ask me when I decided to be a writer I tell them I knew my whole life. They rarely believe me. But as I leaf through early memories I know it is true. By the time I went to high school (I was just twelve) I was passionately committed. Not even poor Sister Paracleta's desperately boring English classes could wrench me from my dream. I was an addict. There were periods when I was forced into being drug-free but sooner or later I was back on my fix.

Sept. 15

The summer is over. Most of it was spent in Montana, running the Ursuline Experience program. Along with that came the final page proofs for *Lady Blackrobes*. And finally came the finished product. *Lady Blackrobes* is actually published with a nice amount of fanfare. But how shall I ever get back to *Encounters*? It seems impossible yet it's unlikely that I have lost my touch. I had it last June. It is in there somewhere. I need time. Time to switch gears and let myself be. I need blurry time when I'm hardly thinking about anything. Even a notch lower than reflective time. I need that but it is hard to come by. So, dear friend, take it easy.

Let yourself sit. No need to produce. It will happen in good time. Wander around in your mind and you will find a place to sit. You don't seem ready to decide what next. Lots of good subjects all neatly written down. Something will fly off the page and into your heart. In its own time. Amen. Amen.

Oct. 20

This is probably my last entry for a while. What does that mean: "for a while?" In a few days I will be having my spinal surgery. I guess I have known for a long time that this would happen ultimately. But I think I had to do the summer and get *Lady Blackrobes* on the road. I have been to two specialists and they have given me the same diagnosis. I did not expect this to be quite so dramatic. I thought they could take care of the spinal stenosis in a couple of days. But alas I have more problems than that. So I will have a "bone fusion" – a six hour surgery followed by months of rehabilitation. OK. I have to do it. Pain is more than I can manage and clearly it is not getting better. I wish I could have brought *Encounters* to some kind of conclusion . . . but 'tis not to be. So I'll tidy up my office, file my pieces of manuscript and hope that in a couple of months I will be able to return. And so as they say on BBC: Goodbye for now!

ENCOUNTERS

# THE WRITING LIFE II

I don't know what would have happened to my writing life had the publication of *Marie of the Incarnation: Mystic and Missionary* not coincided with Vatican II. It seems inevitable that there would have been a clash. With Vatican II the lives of religious women were turned – if not upside down – at least to an unwieldy angle. For myself, as soon as the door was open I joined the crowd jostling their way through to the market place. My goal was not to leave religious life but to find the freedom this new order was offering. I would leave the world of academia behind and become a writer.

I soon found myself milling about randomly with hundreds of other sisters eager to find new ways of living, new fields of service, new channels for living out their vows. We could hardly have been less prepared for this dramatic step. For myself I was determined to leave behind the only course I was prepared for – college teaching – to be the author of books. A writer, yes, but a writer of what? It was a question that left me floundering. To be a writer, to actually be the author of a published book was such a heady experience that I had not looked beyond it. But now I was faced with the practical issues. What would I write? What interested me? What did I want to communicate? Questions, I discovered to my chagrin, that I was not able to answer.

My first topic had been presented to me by religious superiors. Although I certainly would not have admitted it, it was probably in this same spirit that I arrived in John Delaney's office at Doubleday. As Director of Religious Publishing at Doubleday he had accepted my first book and encouraged me to continue writing but I am sure he never expected me to arrive in his office asking, like a school girl, "What shall I write?"

By his role he was necessarily limited to things Catholic and none of his suggestions interested me. I did not want to write a biography of an American bishop or the history of an American cathedral or the influence of sisters on the educational system. In fact I was doing my best to escape from just such subjects, but I had little to offer in their place. John Delaney must be praised for his forbearance. Ultimately we arrived at a compromise. He would offer me a contract for a life of Henri de Navarre, that ambivalent monarch reputed to have commented cynically at his baptism, "Paris is worth a Mass." How Delaney fitted me into his Catholic Division remains a mystery. Perhaps I bewildered him into acquiescence. As for me, sixteenth century France was a period I had researched for my first book, the biography of Marie of the Incarnation, and I was comfortable with it. I was happy, too, at the thought that I could slip away from churchiness into a secular world. At least Henri IV was not a bishop.

After three laborious years *Royal Cousin* was published. As it turned out it wasn't a bad book but it had no place in

Doubleday's Catholic Division. It slipped unnoticed beneath the waves, dying without a single murmur from a reading public. This certainly should have been enough to stop me in my tracks but it seems I was unstoppable. So diffident in so many ways, my confidence in my vocation as a writer was unhesitating. Had I had proper advice, I contended, *Royal Cousin* would never have met such an inglorious end. I was determined that this would not happen again and at once I set about finding a literary agent. And here Lady Luck (or a Guardian Angel) smiled on me. Claire Smith of Harold Ober Associates became my agent and my friend.

In the next ten years she shepherded me through three books: another French biography, *Madame Catherine: The Life of Catherine de Medici*, and two novels, *Seven Sons* and *Accidental Grace*. While they did not make me rich or famous they won me a review in the *New York Times* and a place on Book of the Month Club. I preened with satisfaction – and hoped for more.

At last, eighteen years after my first publication, I made the final leap: I took early retirement from my college teaching and set about becoming a full-time writer. Perhaps it was the radical nature of my decision which set me back on my heels. What on earth was going on? Was this why I had entered religious life – to lock myself up and spend my days before a typewriter (or now a computer)? What did this have to do with my initial consecration? Perhaps I would never have asked the questions if my writing had been going well. But it wasn't. I spent aimless (and lonely) days trying to find a center for my work. I felt like a dog, turning and turning, looking for a spot where he could be at ease. My "mantra" – Full Steam Ahead – had fallen apart. My doubts about my writer's life were augmented when a novel I had poured my heart into could not find a publisher.

While other members of my community went off to teach the ignorant, console the bereft, counsel the confused and feed the hungry, I sat, with the cover still on my computer, looking out at a winter landscape. I who had fled from philosophical (and theological) questions now found myself enmeshed in them. Until now Ernest Hemingway's reputed response to life – I don't give a damn what caused it, I just want to know how to live with it – had seemed eminently satisfying; but now, like my mantra, this, too, had fallen apart. I needed to know what was happening – and why.

Had I somehow abandoned my consecrated religious life to consecrate myself to something other? What was this writing life? Was it something you ticked off on a list of aptitudes? It was more than that, I knew. But what? When I used to question my students about why they wanted to take a course in Short Story Writing, they often said, "I love words." "No, no," I would reply, "that's not enough. Writing is more than that. If it's just a question of loving words, why don't you join the editorial staff of a dictionary? They work with words all the time."

Years ago in graduate school when we were reading the Romantics I came across lines in Wordsworth's *Prelude* which must have impressed me because I have always remembered them.

*I made no vows, but vows were made for me.*
*Else sinning greatly, I should be a dedicated spirit.*

It was a typically Romantic definition of the poet. He

was a man, a superior being, chosen from birth for the exalted mission of providing the world with poetry. My professor gave little shrift to this Wordsworthian babble. The Romantics were in low repute in those days of the New Critics who saw the art of the poet as a matter of craftsmanship rather than pseudo-religious dedication. For Ezra Pound and his followers the poet was The Maker. His highest praise of T.S. Eliot was to pronounce him not a man seized by the gods – as Plato would have it – but simply "the better craftsman."

Was that what I had chosen to be: "the craftsman"? Was this what had drawn me out of the worthwhile work of education, what had led me into a balancing act with my religious consecration? Simply to be a craftsman? Surely that was part of it – the careful adherence to making the sentence right, the panther hunt for the word (to quote Pound again). Yes . . . but this was not all. Perhaps I had been close to the heart of the matter the day I walked into John Delaney's office floundering about in my search for a topic yet convinced that I must be a writer. I knew in some inchoate way that it was not the fervor to communicate a subject but simply the act of writing that had claimed me.

Perhaps the Romantics were not so far from the truth. Perhaps the writer was a "dedicated spirit" – a person gifted and chosen beyond his will. I had no desire to turn the writer's life into a religious vocation and yet . . . . It was clear that it was something beyond the desire to communicate, to structure a narrative, to influence an audience. Something more demanding compelled me: it was the very process itself.

What thrilled me and caught me, filled me with joy (or

anguish) was the process. Putting the thing together, choosing just this phrase, finding just this word, watching the sentence become whole. Reading it over, testing its rhythm, sensing a syllable that kept the song from singing. "Feeling your fingers on the right keys," as I explained to a friend who wanted to understand what it was like to feel yourself writing well.

But even though these reflections nudged me along, the Great Question remained, sweeping over me like a tsunami that might drown me yet. Was my life as a writer inevitably at odds with my life as a consecrated woman? If the writer was a "dedicated spirit" how did this fit with the "dedicated spirit" of my vows? Did they both ask everything? Could they live in amity? Would one always be master with a servant at her feet? And which would be which?

When I had first thought about religious vocation it seemed so paramount (a direct call by God) that my earlier yearnings to be a writer were not in contest. I was in love with the ideal of belonging to God. I wanted to be pure, chaste, poor – and passionate. There was an ascetic pleasure in renouncing my job, my apartment, my freedom. My life as a writer was still too vague to have a strong claim on me. If I thought about it at all it was with a dismissive wave of the hand. There was no dramatic moment when I tore my poems and stories into pieces or – even more grandiosely – cast them into a consuming fire.

Later I read that Gerard Manley Hopkins had, in fact, destroyed his poetry before entering the Jesuits, convinced that the life of the poet had no place in the priesthood. But Hopkins was older, more mature and already a successful poet. His life would always be conflicted. Even after religious obedience had given him back his poetry he still questioned, writing to his friend Robert Bridges that it seemed to him that the vocation of the priest and the vocation of the poet were too "similar" to be able to exist in the same person.

His reflection caught me up short. My immediate reaction was the inverse: far from being similar these vocations were opposites, demanding different ways of being. I remembered Keats with his theory of Negative Capability, that the poet's mind must be a "thoroughfare" – a pathway open to every thought, every sensation, every yearning. But religious instruction had taught me just the opposite: set a guard at every entrance; turn your eyes from allurements; protect your mind from distractions. If Keats was right, the poet and the priest (or any dedicated religious) could never peacefully coexist.

No wonder then that even as I continued my writing life I lived with a sense of shame. When at a workshop or the beginning of a retreat we were asked to introduce ourselves: name, religious community, ministry, my heart froze. Into the bevy of voices: teacher, pastoral assistant, nurse, chaplain came the alien syllables: writer. Sometimes I didn't say it; I fell back on my former position and said "teacher." But that brought its own shame: I had lied; I had used a false passport like a secret agent. Of course I thought of abandoning my writing, of returning to the world of academia. But it didn't take long to realize that this was no solution. I had reached that critical junction: the point of no return.

One day as I looked through notes I had kept from my teaching days, I came across John Gardner's essay, "On

Becoming a Novelist." A writer, he explained, needs "an almost demonic compulsiveness." I knew that compulsiveness. It drove me and directed me. And yet there was my other compulsiveness – the compulsiveness involved in religious consecration. An "angelic" compulsiveness? More and more it seemed to me that they stemmed from the same source. Together – not separately – they were who I was.

But how, I continued to query, was this so? What was the relationship of these two "compulsiveness-es."? I turned of course to Thomas Merton who had often been lost in his own wilderness. "I'm not always sure I'm a monk," he had written, "but I am always sure I am a writer." Was it, I reasoned, because one is prior to the other? That my religious consecration was a mature decision (moved by grace of course) while my writer-life was something I was born with? In this light it was my primary calling, my identification, my DNA, a divine endowment, preceding any decision I might later make. It seemed that I was back to Wordsworth with a new understanding of his lines: "I made no vows but vows were made for me."

The warring elements had begun to fall into place. The more I reflected on the life of contemplation (which my religious consecration called me to) and on my writing-life the more I recognized their identical elements. Both were far from the world of ideas, that alien realm which I had tried to enter but which had never satisfied me. Both called me to a cosmos of limitless quiet, beyond the reach of the rational. Again it was John Gardner who led me deeper: "Those strange moments that overtake you," he wrote, "moments of escape from ordinary time and space – moments no doubt similar to those sought by religious mystics. These moments are the soul of art."

I had known those moments. I had known them as a child, unaware at the time of their source or direction. Later in my religious life I had experienced them again. This time they were more than unexpected flashes; they were the long, slow phrases of a music which drew me into silence. But these gifted moments were not restricted to my life of prayer. I had experienced them as I sat trying to turn an inchoate feeling into a line of prose or poetry. While such moments can never be induced they must be prepared for with a kind of total stillness, that stillness which the Desert Fathers called *hesychia*, the virgin realm of contemplation.

These were the moments that made me whole. They healed my divisions and quieted my anxieties. They were at the very core of my existence. "Absolute attention is prayer," wrote Simone Weil. After all the years of struggle I knew she was right. It was not absolute attention to some attribute or mystery or quality of God that prayer demanded, it was simply "absolute attention." Gerard Manley Hopkins had been right: these vocations of writer and religious were, indeed, similar. But he had not gone far enough. They were not warring vocations. Instead they slipped inside each other like two hands, one warming and cosseting the other. Sometimes one is innermost, sometimes the other. It hardly matters which.

In my office these days there is a small bronze plaque on the wall. "Imagination is evidence of the Divine."

It is the closest I can come to a creedal statement.

ENCOUNTERS

# WALKING TO CATHAY

The winter of 1979 gave me new insight into Herman Melville's famous phrase in the beginning of Moby Dick: "A damp drizzly November in my soul." It had been indeed for me a damp and drizzly season. It was a winter bleak and unending. I felt betrayed by both my worlds – writing as well as teaching.

A few months earlier I had given the completed manuscript of my novel *Accidental Grace* to my agent. She was positive and enthusiastic but the rejection letters that followed undid her encouragement. Had they pointed out a flaw I might be able to correct ("needs a stronger story line" . . . "dialog at times inconsistent with the character") I could have taken heart. But the comments, routinely expressed, struck me with the force of a *coup-de-grâce*: "This well-crafted novel is not right for our list at this time." From such a judgment I could find no escape.

Meanwhile I continued with my college curriculum: two courses in American Lit and a seminar in writing the short story. By that time I should have known that offering a course in Edith Wharton and Henry James was courting disaster.

The students of twenty years earlier who had thrived on the intricacies of Jamesian prose and who had made teaching a joyful exploration had been replaced by a generation unprepared for what I considered the staff of life. It was not so much that we clashed as that we never met.

The fact that religious life as I had known it – and to which I had given my life – was changing dramatically in ways I found questionable did little to temper the winter chill. It was more than feeling cold. I felt frozen, unable to move in any direction. Dante was right when he imaged hell as a kingdom of ice.

I knew I had to do something while I could still crawl and in early January 1980 I wrote to our general government in Rome offering myself for "volunteer service abroad." Since we were an international order I knew there were many schools where teaching English was a high priority. I had the necessary degrees and I was an experienced teacher. Surely I would be wanted somewhere. My letter made it very clear that I had no ability to deal with young children or involve myself in administration. What I had in mind was a professorship in our university in Rio de Janeiro or even better in our college in Australia where I would open eager minds to the elements of American literature.

The reply which reached me in early March was outside my expectations. It thanked me for my generous offer and informed me that the place most in need of my qualifications was Wen Tzao, a college of modern languages, situated in Kaohsiung in southern Taiwan. I caught my breath, folded the letter, stuffed it in my pocket and joined the community for dinner. It took me two days before I regained enough composure to reread the letter. The second reading changed nothing; it simply reaffirmed what I had already read: southern Taiwan was where I was needed.

In the next few days I was able to quiet my initial response ("Thank you; no thank you") to something more balanced. I had, after all, asked a question and I had received an answer. But the answer was far from what I had anticipated. I had been looking for something that would take me from my drab winter chill – a kind of vacation – and I was offered a missionary life instead. I felt angry, resentful – and totally unequal to the task. Suddenly I was confronted by the questions I had been keeping at bay for months. This "dark November in my soul" – what was it? Had it come out of the north blanketing me like a winter storm? Or had I created it out of my dissatisfactions? And, most of all, what was I to do with it? It was clear that I needed time to think and I spent my spring vacation making a retreat in a monastery up the Hudson.

I'm not sure what I intended as the theme of my retreat but in fact I meditated on the undeniable reality that I was growing old. I would soon have my sixtieth birthday – not a great age as age goes these days but I had to face the sobering thought that more than two-thirds of my life had been lived. As I sat looking out at the "lordly Hudson" with its unceasing flow I acknowledged a change in my body. I was slowing down – not by choice, not by desire – but simply by the inevitable motion of change. And yet, paradoxically, as I slowed down, time itself speeded up.

The days, I recognized, seemed to be shorter; the months slipped together. The years no longer stretched before me limitlessly. The time between Christmas and Easter was hardly long enough to change the decorations. The pages of my calendar flipped over before I was ready. In those quiet days of retreat I came to realize that I was reaching a place of inner choice. How would I approach those next twenty years or so of life which modern science almost guaranteed me? Religious life (at least for women) until very recently had no place for "retirement." There was work to be done for as long as our bodies could manage it. Choice, even inner choice, had never been part of the package. But with Vatican II another vista had opened. The image of faithful Sister Polycarp teetering on her cane to greet the fifty-odd children of her first grade class had been variously replaced.

But whatever shifts contemporary life was offering me, in terms of life cycle it was incontrovertibly clear that I was facing autumn. How would I plan for it and for the winter which would inevitably follow? Would I lay in logs for the fire to insure a comfortable winter – or would I continue to live my "outdoor" life, taking my chances with the elements? Although I feared the inevitable chill of winter, I also recognized the danger of a life free from challenge. There was such a thing as too much comfort. I feared to lose energy, to blunt my purpose with too much security. I feared that routine might replace thought, that the daily realities of an elderly life would obscure the mystery and wonder about me. Now as I saw my summer running out, I wanted to gather up all the remaining fragments of my life. I did not want anything to be lost.

Yet at once another drummer called me to his beat. "Let be," said this seductive self. "Let evening move in; there has been enough bright sun and summer. You have stretched your muscles quite enough. Leave the garden; the growing time is over. Come into the house. Light a fire in the hearth. Find a comfortable chair; choose a book. Pull back the curtain from the window if you wish, but moderately so that you view the world distantly, at your leisure." It was a beguiling argument and I felt its allure. Surely it was time for a little comfort.

For the next few weeks I lived with my ambiguities. Ultimately, I came down on the side of Taiwan. What led me to my decision I hardly know. Perhaps it was the sentence in Deuteronomy about choosing life over death or the phrase from St. John's Gospel about darkness and light. In any case, I finally wrote my letter to the president of Wen Tzao College of Modern Languages assuring her that I would be honored to join her faculty.

Although my letter and its gracious reply strengthened my decision, it did little to lessen my fears. Could I, I asked myself, at the age of sixty, having lived all my life in the ordered groves of academe, with a temperament variously described as creative, artistic, moody or unpredictable – could I manage in a country whose name had become a symbol for the mysterious and unknown?

"Far Cathay" was the poet's symbol for the unimaginable. The French captured its elusiveness when they called it the "*Extrême-Orient*." "Digging to China" had been our children's phrase for doing the impossible. "Everyone has his China," was Joan Didion's reflection on our inescapable impulse, our ineluctable dream. For whatever reason, goaded by whatever "ineluctable dream" I was going to Cathay. Would I die out there, I wondered. If not of some exotic disease at least of loneliness – or simple alienation. I comforted my fears with the realization that no matter what happened I couldn't die young.

During those weeks as I made my preparations, I uncovered some comforting facts. The elderly, although burdened by age, are in some ways freer than the young. Despite appearances it is not the young who are able to live free. The young are burdened with anxieties. The young must make decisions that they are often too young to make wisely. They must choose a career, they must prepare themselves professionally, they must build a reputation. Their futures will be determined by how they have spent their youth. But I had reached a stage where I was free. My professional career was established. I had no need to continue to prove myself. Success or failure were now mere surface terms. I could risk everything because the time to amass treasure was over. I had reached that point where it was quite admissible to give everything away. I looked at the approaching winter. I looked at the logs piled at the hearth, at the rocking chair and the afghan folded over its back. I looked at the books yearning to be read – and I found my decision firm at last. Despite the chill, I opened the windows wide, breathed in the invigorating air of late fall, unlatched the door and started walking to Cathay.

ENCOUNTERS

## TO CLIMB A MOUNTAIN

It was not until I traveled into central Taiwan that I understood why western explorers had called the Island "Formosa" – the beautiful island. I had been invited to go with seven members of my Chinese community for a three-day vacation to the mountains. Having no idea of what a Chinese vacation involved I had accepted the invitation gladly. Had I known what lay ahead, my courage would probably have failed for those three days of "vacation" were among the most strenuous of my life.

The first part of our trip was relatively luxurious. It was made in an air-conditioned express bus which took us up the western coast from Kaohsiung through the green farm country of Cia-Yi and into Taichung, seat of the provincial government, where we were to change buses. Now the fun began as we sprinted through the streets of Taichung to catch a "local" bus which would take us along the East-West Highway into the mountains of central Taiwan.

Boarding that bus made boarding a New York City bus at rush hour seem like a fairly tranquil experience. We pushed and scrambled, straddling boxes and sacks, and finally –

exactly on time – we were off. There was no possibility of a seat and for the next two-and-a-half hours I braced my feet and clung to any available object as the bus climbed into the mountains on a road that grew increasingly narrow and winding with sheer mountains rising on one side and ravines plunging on the other.

At one point we lurched wildly and in a desperate effort to retain my balance I found my hand clinging to the hair of a man seated across the aisle next to me. An apology was clearly in order and I groped among my four Chinese phrases (apple, mango, thank you, Lord have mercy) for something appropriate. "Thank you" seemed closest and I tried that. It was accepted with a look of patient bewilderment which told me I was doing nothing to cement US-Taiwanese relations

It was late afternoon before we reached our destination: a youth hostel situated at Tehchi Reservoir, exactly in the center of Taiwan. As we descended from the bus I could see nothing but a small "Welcome" building at the side of the road. But then along the back of this Center were flights of steps leading down along the side of the ravine to a series of buildings large enough to lodge three hundred students. The lodgings were very simple but clean and adequate. The small rooms were arranged Japanese style with tatami mats and heavy quilts. Each room was prepared to accommodate seven people. An additional flight of steps led to the dining room and a simple recreation room, equipped with sturdy wooden furniture and the inevitable TV. For the equivalent of $3.00 US one could get a room for the night plus a more than adequate breakfast and dinner. And all this with one of the most beautiful views I have ever experienced. Directly below the hostel runs the Tachia River – a cool, milky jade-green ribbon – and not fifty yards away the mountains begin to rise, spare slabs of granite at the bottom but then transformed into thick green forest as the mountains towered above the river.

I would have been content to sit there until sunset, comforting my body from the arduous bus trip. But there were definitely other plans. We would go to see the fruit farm, my Chinese companions informed me. There was just time before it grew dark. I searched the mountains on both sides. Where, I asked, could the fruit farm be? Up there, they pointed, up the mountain.

For over an hour I pushed and hauled, slipping on moss-covered stones, grabbing at small trees to help me up the steep uneven path. Finally, breathless and sweating from my exertions, I stood in a little clearing where three men and a woman squatted under a blue and gray tarpaulin sorting pears and apples into large cardboard boxes. Above me, on all sides, stretched the orchards, terraced along the mountain, growing at precarious angles where no fruit trees should rightly be expected to grow. As I stood, other workers came in from the orchards, their heads covered by the traditional "Chinese coolie" hats, poles across their shoulders from which hung huge baskets heaped high with fruit. I stood bemused. Where was I, I wondered. And was I really witness to this strange scene of primitive labor and successful commercial enterprise? The spell was broken by Sister Mei-lan who offered me an apple. "Eat," she said, smiling proudly, "native-born apple."

Apples are not native to Taiwan which abounds in all kinds of tropical fruits – mango, papaya, guava, melons. Most of the Island is too warm to produce apples. Some thirty years ago, however, the government in an effort to provide work for the demobilized military personnel encouraged the retirees to go to the mountains and begin farming. The climate, it was discovered, was perfect for apples and pears. For the next twenty years the steep hillsides were perseveringly cleared and cultivated until today there are miles and miles of orchards producing "native-born" apples and pears of remarkable quality.

How was it possible, I wondered, as I tried to reconstruct those first efforts to clear the land of those dense forests, to move the logs, to prepare that tough virgin soil, to terrace it, to plant those first apple and pear trees and to arrange a system of irrigation. How was it possible? And with what tools had the miracle been accomplished? It was clear that no heavy equipment had made its way up those mountains. Looking around I could see nothing but some shovels, a pick, a small cart, dozens of sturdy baskets, and a large supply of cardboards boxes, neatly stamped, which would eventually find their way down the mountain and into the markets of Taiwan and beyond. Even the final state of getting the fruit down the mountain is a manual task. Although in some sections cables have been installed to lift the boxes down to the roadside where they can be picked up by trucks, this is still the exception. Most of the fruit is carted down those treacherous paths by means of strong and persevering backs and arms.

How was it possible? I had been plagued during my first weeks in Taiwan by what seemed to me the most hopeless inefficiency. Everything looked ramshackle. Men repaired the highways with small inefficient shovels. Women swept their boxlike houses with broken or inadequate brooms.

Loads were carried through the streets in listing carts pulled by ancient rusty bicycles. Pipes seemed always to be held together by cloth or wire. Overhead wires looped and swayed drunkenly. How, I had wondered, was it possible for anything ever to get accomplished in such a system.

Now, as I sat on a small stool – graciously provided for the feeble American – eating my native-born apple, I had to revise my thinking. Clearly it was possible. Not by any standard I had ever lived with. But it was possible. I recalled a little exchange on our way up to the orchard. At one point I had collapsed on the side of the path, shaking my head and waving my companions on. But Mei-lan would have none of it. Defeat was something she would not accept. "You come," she said, pulling my arm. I shook my head again. "I can't," I pleaded, "too old." "You come," she repeated, tightening her grasp on my arm. So: I was to take part in the Long March! I got to my feet. "Slow," said Mei-lan, "no need hurry. Little bit, then little bit. Pretty soon at top."

Yes. Clearly, that's the way it's done. Little bit, then little bit and you've cleared a forest, planted an orchard, established an industry. It is, I suspect, the only answer I will ever get to my question: how is it possible?

I slept that night – well, but not long enough. We were up next morning before five to see the sunrise and to sing – quite literally – the joy of being alive. Breakfast that morning betrayed me. When we came to the dining hall the liquid breakfast rice was already steaming away and the wooden table was filled with a variety of small dishes to flavor the rice. Most of these things I had already learned to be wary of. My western morning-stomach, brought up on black coffee and toast, flinched before such delicacies as pickled eggs. But there at the side, to my delight, was a dish of something that was surely coarse brown sugar. What could be more delicious on a cold morning in the mountains than hot rice and brown sugar! Only too late – much too late – did I discover that the "brown sugar" was, in fact, fish powder.

By eight o'clock we were off again – this time to Lishan (Pear Mountain), originally one of the chief areas for the Tayal tribe of aborigines but now a youth resort from which one can climb higher into the mountains. And climb we did. The first part of the climb was along a well-traveled road. After a few miles we were fortunate in getting a ride from an obliging man with a truck who dropped us about halfway up the mountain at a little tourist station, consisting of a shrine to Confucius, a few rustic seats and a very primitive WC.

I was the first one out of the truck and as I turned I found myself face to face with a tall elderly Chinese who bowed at me graciously. "For whom are you looking?" he asked me in perfect English. Surely this was a line from a play I hadn't read. Who could I possibly be looking for in the mountains of Taiwan? There must, I thought, be some wonderful mystical answer: Lao-Tzu? Confucius? The Way of Truth? Surely not Godot again! Only later did I learn that this was the only English phrase this Chinese gentleman knew, a phrase which he had little opportunity to use since few Westerners penetrate to Lishan. My presence provided him with an unexpected and joyful occasion. And like a good Chinese he had not let the opportunity slip!

For the next few hours we continued gradually upward with the comfort of a real road under our feet. At one point a truck loaded with vegetables stopped and offered us a ride. Somehow we managed to scramble in among the Chinese cabbages and the truck continued slowly climbing higher and higher until the mountain leveled out and we were on a grassy plain overlooking the world. There were yellow and purple wild flowers everywhere and a few pines rising dark above the horizon. Two yellow finches swooped and dived from tree to tree. Everywhere black and orange butterflies, bigger than humming birds, rose from the grass, arced in short flights and then settled down again. It was only mid-afternoon but already the mist – purple-gray – was beginning to settle over the western mountain.

We sat for a while, meeting silence with silence. It was the silence of exhaustion but it was more: it was the silence of exaltation. We had reached the top of the mountain.

The next morning we started back to Kaohsiung. The return bus was quiet and surprisingly empty. I dozed a good part of the way. From time to time I stretched my aching muscles. Mei-lan reached out her hand to cover mine. It looked very thin and brown and graceful next to my heavy, freckled one. "You have climb mountain," she said and smiled. I nodded, smiling back. So I had. Despite all my hesitation, all my misgiving, all my inexperience, I had climbed the mountain. I closed my eyes, remembering... "little bit... then little bit".... And then I dozed again.

# ENCOUNTERS

## SWATCHES FROM A TAIWAN DIARY

*During the two years I taught English in a language college in southern Taiwan I came close to abandoning my dream of writing. Although so much around me was richly interesting I could not find time or energy to explore it and capture it in words. The number of my teaching hours, the large registration in my classes, the constant written assignments to be corrected left me exhausted and angry. The best I could do was keep a diary, scribbling some of the events of the day with the hope that in time I would be able to explore them further and translate them into acceptable English. "Swatches" I called them – small pieces cut from a larger fabric catching the pattern and the colors of the whole.*

\* \* \*

Fuss and flurry in the French Department!

It goes like this: a teacher in the French Department is being married and it is customary to present a "red envelope" – filled with money of course. So carefully, very carefully, the members of the French Department figured out how much each one should give to reach a certain sum. But, alas, one new teacher, recently arrived from France, did not understand the arrangements and had bought a little gift on her own instead of making the expected contribution. Consequently, when the sums were added they did not reach the total projected.

Pandemonium! Why? Not because the total was less than anticipated but because the number of dollars, in conjunction with the date of the wedding, turned out to be an unlucky number. What to do? Finally, after much discussion, the French lady agreed to give something extra, thus avoiding the unlucky number. And now all is well.

* * *

From our roof I can see in the distance a tall white building with a large cross. It is a leprosarium. I have seen a leper only once. He came into the market one day begging. He was filthy with the filth no simple shower could remove. A ragged blanket covered his shoulders and his toes and part of his face were eaten away. People skirted him, backing away, pointing their fingers and shouting in derision. "Why," I asked Ellen Mary who was with me, "Why does he come here? Can the leprosarium be that bad?" She shrugged. "Probably not but this is his hour of freedom." I watched him being jeered and repulsed, enduring it all for this infinitely precious moment of freedom.

* * *

Sometimes even in the midst of so much busi-ness, I dream about the publication of my book. *Accidental Grace* has finally found a publisher after months of uncertainty. I would love to be home, in touch with my agent, having lunch with my editor. Instead I am here thousands of miles away dependent on the power of e-mail. Sometimes in the evening I sit in my room trying to remember favorite passages to recite to myself. Sometimes I wonder if I would have been a really good novelist had I given myself to that. That is really my sacrifice: not a husband or children or a home – not even human love. My deepest drive – even here in this bewildering land – is to be a good writer.

\* \* \*

This is the story of Ursula. Ursula is her English name; I have not yet mastered her Chinese name. She is a fifth year student, almost twenty years old – or perhaps more because she has already missed a year of school. She is so small-boned that she is like a very shy bird. She is a poor student which does not help her shyness. She watches me carefully but has never spoken to me until last week when she followed me out of class to ask a question.

We had been reading Thomas Hardy's *Tess of the Durbervilles* – a struggle for them in every way. The choice of books for them to read is limited and often less than appropriate but I forge on, discussing the attitude toward women in the nineteenth century and contrasting it with their own world. "Sister," asked Ursula stumbling over the English words, "my father say when I get marry I must be like clear water to my husband's stroke." A pause and then her question: "You believe this, Sister?" I wanted to cry. I wanted to tell this beautiful, wistful child that she has a heart and soul of her own. That no man – neither father nor husband – has a right to shape and possess her. But I must be careful. I am a Western woman in an Eastern world. I cannot teach

Ursula more than she can bear. I watch her trying to come awake and alive to herself and try to support this new life without forcing it beyond its capacity

As Ursula walked away, I knew that old China, with its tradition of bound feet, was still alive.

\* \* \*

Taiwan is an arid land for me. It rarely rains and it is a mystery to me how the plants grow – a heavy mass of bougainvillea and stalky, dusty poinsettias along the roadside. There is something harsh even among the blooms. They do not satisfy me. My heart has been yearning toward sweetness for a long time now – not a good word, I know, but I cannot find a better. I long for music, a sweet Mozart melody or a gentle, loving touch of God's presence. How long will I have to wait, I wonder.

Sunday at Mass, as clear as sunlight, this came to me. "That way will not come again; you have moved to another place." "Oh, I see," I said. So, no more waiting for sweetness. Perhaps I shall learn to drink a pure, dry wine instead.

\* \* \*

In Zen before you begin your prayer you are taught to say, "Now I must die the great death." To put to death all that will come between you and your silence.

\* \* \*

The other day as my class studied a short story I pointed out that the heroine must either marry a man she didn't love or return home disgraced. "Do you see any other option?" I asked. "Yes," answered Mei-lan, "she can suicide." To which many nodded in approval. Suicide among the young is not unusual here. It is not caused so much by despair or severe depression. A single instance of humiliation is often enough. The daily paper carried the case of a young man slapped by his mother in front of his friends. This insult to his manhood was enough to cause his death. The number of suicides increases during the period of university examinations. To fail is to "lose face," an unendurable humiliation for the Chinese.

* * *

It is Christianity that christianizes, I am learning. Simply that. And that is not tautological but an expression of truth. Baptism is the beginning, the inexpressible seed of life. But it is the total Christian experience that awakens and vivifies that larger dimension which perhaps I can call the social Christian soul. I learn this from living in a culture outside Christianity.

* * *

I have just learned that Father Gutienz, an Austrian Jesuit, who has come a few times for talk, confession, etc., cannot come for the rest of this year. And thus is removed my last spiritual prop. Father Fong speaks Chinese; Father Réal speaks French and understands Chinese . . . . I speak English . . . but to whom?

* * *

Let me say something of Father Hou. Father Hou fled Mainland China thirty years ago with the coming of the Communists. He is only in his sixties but he is an old, old man. Now he has a tiny parish in Taipei. His "church" is a room off the lobby of an apartment house. It is small and crowded with cumbersome wooden pews, vases of dusty artificial flowers, a large old-fashioned altar and ragged drapes. Father Hou is so thin that he looks two dimensional, with his black-green cassock hanging on him like a paper-doll cut-out. Every day he says a requiem in black vestments with his back to the congregation in the pre-Vatican II mode. He lives in a world that has passed away. On one wall is a bulletin board covered with Chinese memorial cards – old friends killed in the war, priests dead in Chinese prisons. His Mass is a chilling experience. It is always a requiem as though he is still waiting for a sign that Jesus has risen from the dead.

* * *

I have formed an extraordinary attachment to Boiled Egg. Boiled Egg, you see, is invulnerable. You can't put garlic in it; you can't impregnate it with ginger root. You can, of course, for Special Occasion, bury it or plunge it into a barrel of briny liquid to make it more precious. But ordinarily Boiled Egg remains impregnable: pure and inviolate.

* * *

This evening we brave the heat of the community room to watch the old Ronald Coleman film, *A Tale of Two Cities*. It is bewildering to listen to those elegant English voices while the lizards make their strange mechanical little barks around us. Clearly the language is too difficult for many of the community but they persevere. During the citizens' trial of Darnay I sense a change of atmosphere and when I look around I notice a tension and fear that seem out of all proportion to the suspense created by the film. Then I realize. Of course! Most people in the room have had some equivalent experience. Dorothy's family lost everything and only escaped with their lives. Li has memories of her grandmother being subjected to the water torture from which she never recovered. Julie's family moved constantly in an effort to keep a few miles ahead of the Communists; and Augustine herself has been tried and imprisoned by a people's court. For me it is only a drama, an interesting episode in an old sentimental movie. Clearly I am an alien.

* * *

I am learning to take the zodiac signs more seriously.

The zodiac sign of the snake is a very bad sign. The snake is sly, clever, treacherous and unpredictable. Women who are pregnant during the year of the snake go through great anguish. The year of the tiger is also a problem. One of my students told me that because her zodiac sign was a tiger she could not attend her sister's wedding. No tiger should ever attend a wedding. The tiger can do harm to the bride!

* * *

The other night a young French pianist performed at our new Cultural Center. She played Haydn, Rachmaninoff, Ravel. It was not my favorite music ( I would have chosen Mahler or Mozart) but it moved me to tears. She wasn't magnificent but she was good. My reaction: close to anger that she should come with her gifts, invade my world and then smile and say goodbye . . . leaving me. How far away I am from everything I have called "my life." Is that a note of regret, Irene? No, I don't think so. Just a little reality check that comes from time to time.

# SWATCHES FROM A TAIWAN DIARY

* * *

Along with my daily journal I have kept a notebook of items culled from student papers. Some of them are quite wonderful:

> She took the letter and through it to the flour
>
> In her sympathy she took the cat and dried it up
>
> He formed an affection for a beautiful typewriter that worked in his office
>
> The United States is a demoncracy with tree branches of government
>
> Spain is a very Christian country in which religious men live together in moanasteris and religious women live in convents for cloistered nuts

When asked to list a book by Steinbeck or Hemingway, we have:

> The Angry Grape
>
> The Furious Grape
>
> The Man and the Mouse
>
> Fairwell to the Army
>
> Farewell to my Arms

* * *

Today the Summer Session, a four week program for Taiwanese teachers of English, has come to an end and the members of the session invite us to a concluding program. In addition to speeches of gratitude comes a program of dances, songs, recitals. The MC is a young man with the English name of Daniel. Chinese modesty has passed Daniel by and he speaks volubly of his musical aspirations and his acceptance into a language program at Fort Worth, Texas. Since he has a severe problem in pronouncing "Fort Worth" I entertain misgivings about his successful arrival. Daniel begins his selection with "O Sole Mio" to which the audience responds rapturously. To sing! Yes, but to sing in Italian is overwhelming! But it was Daniel's second selection which brought his audience to his side. This was a Taiwanese folk-song with the improbable refrain, "Do not eat the goldfish at the bottom of the wine bowl." It was a rousing conclusion with Daniel's fellow students singing and clapping in rhythm, leaving me with my persistent question: what has happened to my image of the quiet inscrutable Chinese?

\* \* \*

A typhoon warning has been out for several days. The word strikes terror to my heart. I remember learning in a linguistic course that typhoon is one of the few Chinese words to come into English. Tai-Fung: the Great Wind. Well, the Great Wind has diddled about in the Philippines and only this afternoon has it picked up speed and headed for southern Taiwan. Kaohsiung is often badly hit since we are a coastal city. Sister Cecilia tells me that at their last big typhoon the whole roof of the school was ripped off – "it blew away like pieces of paper." By evening the typhoon arrived and we had a wild night. Furious winds with a very special kind of "whoosh." At first I thought I could leave my window open a crack but it was soon clear that everything had to be battened down. When the rain came it was like standing behind Niagara Falls. By morning things had quieted down a bit but throughout the day the rains and winds have remained fierce and we are without electricity.

# SWATCHES FROM A TAIWAN DIARY

\* \* \*

Last night was "Things that go bump in the night" night. My fan was so noisy that I finally turned it off. About 1:30 I woke steaming and bitten alive despite my mosquito net. I dozed off again but in my restlessness pulled down part of the net on top of me and woke from a dream of being suffocated. I got up, put on the light, tried to fix the wretched net only to discover a multitude of tiny gnats snuggled up in my bed. Meanwhile a lizard, nervous from all the activity, had fallen with a plop on my desk but just as I was about to get back into bed I spied the largest, furriest spider I have ever seen scurrying toward the door. So much for sleep. I tucked myself in with my crippled mosquito net and read last month's *TIME* from cover to cover. This morning Angela, having heard of my troubles, brought me a new mosquito net and a can of insect spray. "Something scare you, you shoot," she instructed.

\* \* \*

Someone told me of asking directions of a Chinese person who attempted to answer in English. "Take this street," he said. "Go until you come to a spoon in the road."

ENCOUNTERS

# PRACTICING THE GREAT RESOLVE

Our long vacation for Chinese New Year provided me with an opening to make a Zen retreat. I pounced on the opportunity. I wish I could say that I was motivated by a pure desire to deepen and expand my spirituality but my motive was nothing so elevated. The high purpose which had brought me to Taiwan was getting shredded. I had come to rededicate my life to God, to abandon all the comforts and securities with which I had surrounded myself and renew that ultimate abandonment which had originally led me to religious life. It was a glorious ideal but there is nothing like unremitting work and a torrid climate to melt down ideals.

I was tired: tired of the staccato sounds of Mandarin, of endless hours of correcting papers, of the unremitting demands of Chinese red tape. My dreams of China were, I was discovering, far from the actuality. My vision had been shaped by the Chinese collections of the Metropolitan Museum of Art: images of pagodas, rising in red and gold splendor, of Chinese vases with delicate hand-painted orchids and chrysanthemums, of scrolls with tall pines arching over a mountain stream where a small wooden hut housed a poet-scholar. My daily life presented me with a very different reality. I had yet to see a graceful pagoda; most of the buildings I had seen were unadorned cement structures.

From the beginning Taiwan had bewildered me. There was nothing in my ride from the Taipei airport which spoke of the calm and serenity I had associated with Confucius and his descendents. The airport bus was crowded and noisy with music blaring Taiwanese rock – a terrible mixture of western beat and incomprehensible Chinese lyrics. Although it was already dark, the streets were teeming with activity. Motorcycles, Hondas, small cars roared by at break-neck speed, horns in constant use. Bicycles and pedestrians weaved in and out, guided by some inner vision which I did not share. Although I could not see an inch of space anywhere, yet on every corner were carts and stands – mobile or stationary – loaded with food. We careened through the streets, missing by inches other cars, carts heaped with cabbages or live chickens, trucks listing with heavy loads – and pedestrians, fleet-footed and sure-footed, requisites for staying alive on these tumultuous streets.

I looked in vain for something "Chinese" – for something beautiful. Even in the poorest parts of Mexico I had found something beautiful: carts of oranges heaped in lovely designs, colorful rebozos cloaking the women's heads, even the old drunks holding themselves as erect as heroes. But on that first night in Taiwan I could see nothing beautiful. The next day I wrote in my diary; "If I die on this island, the cause will be ugliness."

In time, of course, I did find pagodas. I found Tao temples and the peaceful reaches of a Buddhist monastery. And closer to home I found the architecture of the administration building at Wen Tzao which embodied all my dreams of Chinese elegance. But even so, Taiwan, I found, was far from my dream of a land where people were soft-spoken, quiet in their movements, slow and contemplative in speech. The Chinese I dealt with were quick, noisy, aggressive, and ambitious. My students were a delight to teach: attentive, alert, responsive but far from contemplative. I wanted something else. I wanted something quiet and beautiful. Whether a Zen retreat would fill the bill I didn't know, but I was willing to give it a go.

The retreat was to be given at a convent of Chinese Franciscan Missionaries of Mary in Tainan, a city about an hour's drive north of my home in Kaohsiung. Tainan, unlike the industrialized city I had grown used to, was one of the island's most historic sites. Once the capital of Taiwan, it still bore the marks of its former rulers: the Dutch, the Portuguese, the Japanese. I had visited the city earlier and loved the quieter pace and the reverence for its history.

The Franciscans had chosen an ideal spot for their Spiritual Center, sufficiently distanced from the city, with extensive grounds which in this cool winter season were green and flourishing. The architecture was western but everything else had a distinctly oriental flavor. I was led to my room by a novice who did her best to say "Welcome," a strange garbled sound since both the "w" and the "l" were beyond her. With the exception of a German Benedictine priest I was the only Westerner participating in the retreat. This time my nationality was in my favor. I was led not to the large dormitory but to a single room with a bathroom of my own with (could I believe it?) a western style toilet – and an Irish blessing hanging over my desk.

Clearly, English was not spoken here but I understood that we were to change to our "Zen clothes" – loose pants and top – and proceed to the Zendo by 4:30. And so began this life-changing experience. My recollection of the Zendo is of a large bare room, without images, without windows – a womb in which we were to "live and move and have our being" for the next week. I suppose there must have been windows some place but I know that during the entire experience I was spared every distraction from an outside world. Just once, in a desperate moment, I gulped down my lunch, found my way to a back door and bolted into a beautiful garden surrounded by sheltering conifers. For a few stolen moments I breathed in the greenness of it all before returning to the Zendo.

That first night we stood awkwardly, in silence, until we were directed toward the Zen pillows, set in a horseshoe shape. Here we were to sit, facing the walls, each pillow no more than two feet apart and yet with measureless inner distance from each other. We would never see each other's faces.

The Zendo, I would later learn, had originally been the convent chapel. But these Chinese Franciscans, had set themselves a courageous task. After generations of training in Western spirituality there was a movement developing among the young to find a spirituality more consonant with Chinese spirit and tradition. With this as their goal, the sisters, while maintaining their Benedictine identity, made the decision to adapt Zen as their way of prayer. Their chapel had been converted into a Zendo. Pews had been removed and replaced by Zen pillows. Although the Mass and the Divine Office were still the essential part of their spirituality, many of the trappings associated with Christianity were missing. Most art throughout the monastery was Chinese and the Zendo itself was devoid of images.

The Master who would guide us for the next week was Father J. K. Kadowaki, a Japanese Jesuit, stationed in Tokyo. He had recently completed his doctoral studies at Fordham University in New York City and, as a consequence, was fluent in English; but, explained the Japanese sister, whom he had brought to assist him, he knew no Chinese. Since most of the participants were assumed to know some English and since language was only a minor element in our Zen experience, all conferences would be given in English. My heart leaped with relief but as I stole a glance to left and right the dismayed faces gave me the distinct feeling that Father Kodawaki and I would be having private conversations most of the time.

Following this brief introduction we proceeded to the dining room for a simple supper – in silence – and returned at 7:00 to the Zendo. Father Kodawaki made his appearance at last – a small beardless man wrapped in a black kimono. He motioned us to take our places on our pillows and observed as we tried awkwardly to tuck our legs into some position vaguely resembling the lotus posture. Those long legs which had stood me in such good stead all my life were now my nemesis.

Slowly, and with excellent enunciation, he explained that since we were novices he would permit us to sit half-lotus since full lotus would be too difficult for us It didn't take me long to realize, however, that his concession was very minor indeed. After no more than a quarter of an hour I was absorbed in pain. Somewhere off in the distance Father Kodawaki spoke on, but close at hand the shriek of my muscles drowned out everything but their cry for mercy. In the morning, he explained, as he dismissed us at last, the bell will ring at 5:30. We will gather in the Zendo for morning meditation followed by Mass. Since this is not an experience of pure Zen but of Christian Zen God will play a part in our *sesshin*.

Before I went to bed I looked over the schedule which had been left in my room. Between the hours of 6:00 a.m. and 9:00 p.m. we would sit, walk, breathe. We would have two thirty minute periods for lunch and supper; two ten minute periods for "free time" and an hour and a half for afternoon siesta. This was serious stuff.

Yet the next morning it was not austerity that Father Kodawaki preached to us but harmony. The discipline which Zen demanded was never an end in itself but a means of balancing those two basic elements of body and spirit, he explained. We began by a prayer to the Holy Spirit: "Holy Spirit, come to enlighten us to the importance of the body in our spiritual lives." The importance of the body. Perhaps by temperament and certainly by training I had come to think of the body as the element to be subjugated, even cast aside since it was generally a cause of sin. Gluttony, lust, sloth were "sins of the flesh." Even gentle St. Francis had referred to his body as "Brother Ass." And now we were being invited to bring Brother Ass out of the barnyard and into the chapel. "Before each meditation, we must recall the mind to the body so that they are brought into harmony."

# ENCOUNTERS

Westerners, the Master continued, see everything in a kind of dualism. Zen will help us to understand ourselves in a holistic, unified way. "I think, therefore I am," wrote the western philosopher Descartes as though our thinking is the very fabric of our being. But Zen is not concerned with thoughts. Zen will not give you new ideas; Zen will bring you to a new way of being. But slowly, very slowly ... not through thinking ... through sitting, through breathing. Shallow breathing will not help. Our breathing must be from our *hara* – that deep place in our body. Do not think of controlling your breathing, rather of assisting it. Breathing has its own nature, its own rhythm. We help it by awareness.

The Master's voice stopped and we were left on our own ... to sit ... to breathe ... and to suffer the excruciating pain of the half-lotus.

We met several times that day, Father Kodawaki's soft voice leading us toward harmony, toward silence. The pain of my legs did not diminish and yet each time I thought I could not continue I discovered that there was a way beyond endurance. "You do not fight the pain," he guided us. "You accept it gently as part of yourself, not as an enemy." Pain not as an enemy? Was it possible? Determined to try, I began to work at incorporating my pain into my breathing. When the meditation session ended I was still in place, still sitting on my cushion, my back erect, my breathing deep.

Not everyone was as fortunate and I could hear about me rustlings of legs being surreptitiously moved, sighs close to groans indicating that even those small Chinese bodies were finding the discipline difficult. For all Father Kodawaki's gentle manner, he was a Master in the tradition.

## PRACTICING THE GREAT RESOLVE

In the unbroken silence the slightest bodily movement was perceptible, and as the tall angular Benedictine priest shifted his legs, the Master's voice rang out: "There is to be no movement during the meditation. Movement is not a physical need; it comes from a restless, unstable spirit." I had discovered earlier on that any effort at movement as you sat half-lotus was worse than useless. It was like a very clever torture. When you try to relieve your leg you pull a muscle in your back. When you try to ease your toes you tighten your thighs.

The amazing thing, I was discovering, was that despite the rigors of the day I was not exhausted. I was glad to get to my bed at night but during the day I found myself energetic and alert. A few times, quite unexpectedly, the sense of God's presence slipped through my pain and reached my consciousness. In some way I had never experienced before I found myself "awakened." This did not diminish my pain nor interrupt my breathing but seemed rather to deepen it and emphasize my dependence on that slow, profound rhythm that welled from my *hara*.

Zen meditation is often called The Great Death, the Master explained to us. In this meditation we must divest ourselves of everything – everything we think of as our life. To sit Zen is to sit in total silence. It is not enough to separate ourselves from exterior noise. It is the silence of the spirit and the quiet of the body that matters. Thus we do not move restlessly, shifting about to seek a more comfortable position. But even more important is the silence of the spirit. We must divest ourselves not only of spoken words but of those silent words, that inner conversation in which we are always engaged. Our images, too, those subtle means of communication, must be sacrificed. When you close your eyes there must be nothing there, only the rhythm of your breathing. Each time you begin your meditation you must have this Great Resolve, this absolute determination to shed everything that could shield you from the power of silence.

For the rest of the day that single phrase dominated me: The Great Resolve, the absolute determination . . . .

On the fifth day we were introduced to that point of discipline called "Receiving The Stroke." The Stroke. I had heard of The Stroke but had presumed it to be one of those mythic elements of Zen – gossiped about by those who knew little and invested with a sort of magic cruelty. But here I was, listening to the Master's quiet precise voice describing what I had cursorily dismissed.

The ritual of The Stroke, he explained, was based upon the basic element of Zen teaching: the harmony of body and spirit. What strengthens the body strengthens the spirit. Every physical act is a spiritual act. People ignorant of Zen think of it as a matter of nothingness. The exact opposite is true. In Zen practice everything is raised to consciousness. On the deepest level the entire person is brought totally alive, vivified by bodily awakening. The Stroke was a ritual to bring us to this awakening.

Since, he continued, we were novices, The Stroke will be optional during this retreat. We will continue to sit on our pillows as usual. Should we wish to receive The Stroke we will join our hands as though in prayer. Then The Master will stand behind us and both will bow in unison. The disciple will then bend over with his hands touching the ground and his back rounded, waiting for The Stroke. The stroke is administered through a flat piece of wood, about three feet long and six inches wide. The disciple is struck on the bone, about eight inches below the neck – the center of the nervous system. The pain is momentary but the sound is fearful. In that silent room the crack of wood against bone is shattering. Immediately following The Stroke the disciple sits erect and bows with the Master.

For me the result was a tingling which reached all through my body like an electric shock. Yes, I felt revitalized and awakened. What had seemed impossibly difficult had become desirable and possible. I knew that my intention in engaging in this ritual was far from "pure." I had done it largely through curiosity. But even so the ritual had achieved its result in a way I could never explain. In some mysterious way I did not understand, I had been awakened. As the Master had instructed us: every physical act is a spiritual act. I was learning to give Brother Ass his rightful position.

On the final day I had my opportunity for a conference with the Master. As usual I put too much emphasis on this single event. Although I had so much to ask I found I could say very little. I could not turn the profound reaches of this experience into words. I groped for a question but failed to be articulate. I thanked him. I asked him if he thought at my age I was capable of engaging seriously in Zen. I received a prompt nod and a quizzical smile. I wanted to say: How? How will I hold on to all this in my world of Cartesian logic? How will my prayer adjust to this new and profound discipline? How will I live with this new vision of reality? But I said nothing. In my heart (or maybe in my *hara*) I knew that even if I asked the questions he would not answer them. He would tell me to practice the Great Resolve, to observe the discipline. To live.

# ENCOUNTERS

After the final conference Father Wei who had made the *sesshin* and lived close to me in Kaohsiung offered me a ride home. It had been clear to me during the week that Father Wei was not taking this experience too seriously. I hesitated. For a moment I almost said I would take the bus but the convenience of a ride to my door proved too much of a temptation. I consoled myself with the thought that since Father Wei knew very little English we would not have much conversation on the way. In this I was right. But I had not accounted for the fact that Father Wei had a car radio. All the way along the tumultuous Taiwan roads Father Wei treated me to a kind of Chinese rock. When the ceaseless honking of car horns became difficult he smiled happily and turned up the volume.

Supper was long over when I arrived home and I could go straight to my room with a minimum of conversation. I closed the door and looked out into the dark courtyard, the pavement shiny in the rain. I had brought home a treasure without shape or weight. How would I protect it? I looked around for something that might be fashioned into a Zen pillow. I took a quilt from my closet and shaped it into a twenty-inch square. I turned off the light and folded myself into the half-lotus. That night I began my practice of The Great Resolve.

Coda:

*For the next twenty-one months that I lived in Taiwan I was faithful to my Great Resolve. When I moved back to the States I wavered for a while as I adjusted to another society. In time, however, I resumed my practice, even buying a proper Zen pillow in a little store down in Greenwich Village. Some of the tenets* of Zen, I was discovering, were finding their way into Western spirituality. The need for meditation, reflection, contemplation was becoming more and more obvious as the world grew busier and noisier. Christian meditation was beginning to develop methods such as Centering Prayer which incorporated the inner silence of Zen. I found it a perfect harmony.

In time, even the half-lotus became more difficult than my ageing bones could manage and I adjusted my sitting to something more practical. But those deep hara breaths continued to sustain me. There are, of course, those bleak times when I long to have a Master who will deliver The Stroke and awaken me, body and spirit, to "the power of silence."

I suppose that in the Christian dispensation I would say that I long for grace.

ENCOUNTERS

# THE BUDDHIST NUN AND THE "HOLY FATHER"

Shortly before leaving Taiwan for my return to the States, I was asked where I would like to go on a weekend vacation as a kind of farewell to the island. Without a moment's hesitation, I answered, "Tienhsiang." My instant response surprised me. I had not realized that this small village in the eastern mountains had impressed me so deeply. I had been there only once before in November of my first year at Wen Tzao. The college had had a long weekend and in company with two Chinese sisters, Mei-lan and Su-ling, I had flown to Hwalien, the coastal city where French Ursuline missionaries had established their first school in Taiwan.

Because Hwalien was on the ocean and was also the gateway to the central mountains, it had taken on the coloring of a resort town, especially popular with the Japanese. The crowds of Japanese tourists astonished me since the Japanese occupation of the Island still rankled in the memories of many Chinese. My plane was peopled mostly by a Japanese tour group – a determined crowd who, despite our seat reservations, acted as though being first to board was a matter of samurai honor. It was a pleasant flight of about forty minutes with blue sky and jagged mountain peaks visible during most of the trip. Although Hwalien and Kaohsiung are only about two hundred miles apart, because of the condition of the roads it would have taken all day to cover the distance by bus and even longer by train.

The convent and school in Hwalien had remained French to an astounding degree. The buildings themselves followed the pattern of a French cloistered school: three long wings with an inner courtyard. The whole was called "Stella Maris" (Star of the Sea) in memory of the original school in China which had been lost to the Communist incursion. But Chinese influence has also made its mark and instead of the meticulous order of the French, here school rooms, dormitory space, refectory, nuns' rooms were randomly situated making it well nigh impossible to find your way around.

After dinner I was collared by an old French nun with a hearty red face and a minimum number of teeth who regaled me for more than an hour about her childhood in Normandy. She was eighty-four, she told me proudly, and a "real" missionary who had been on the missions for sixty years without ever returning to France. Yet as I watched her gestures and listened to the tenor of her narrative, it was clear that, in fact, she had never left France. She had simply brought her homeland with her, like a tent which she could spread out and shelter under wherever she lived.

The following morning, accompanied by Mei-lan and Su-ling, I left for a two-day trip into the mountains. The school minibus was to take us to Tienhsiang where we would stay overnight, returning to Hwalien by public bus.

# ENCOUNTERS

As we drove north, the light rain stopped but the mountains remained half-covered in mist. The atmosphere was somber and the three of us were mostly silent. The scenery had become increasingly wild and forbidding and the mist made everything seem unreal. On one side was a deep rocky gorge with a shallow stream plunging in a white cascade over the stones; on the other, the sheer mountains rose uncompromisingly. I tried not to notice how narrow the road was and how uneven in places.

Suddenly we entered a tunnel and despite our headlights we could see very little. Then just before we emerged into the patch of daylight I saw a large crane-like machine blocking our exit. Our driver jammed on his brakes and leaned out to see what was going on. There followed a great shouted (as always!) conversation and then Su-ling nodded and turned to me: "They bomb mountain," she said. At once there was a series of bone-rattling detonations. There in that tunnel it seemed to me that the world was lifting up only to come down in small pieces on my head. My instant thought was that the Chinese from the Mainland had come at last. But as we soon learned, it was not "bombing" we had been subjected to but "blasting." We had mistakenly intruded upon a crew which was widening the road just a hundred feet ahead of us. All vehicles were to have been stopped at the entrance to the tunnel but somehow we had slipped by. The man in charge had gone off – perhaps for his morning tea – and left his post unattended. Thank God for the machine at the end of the tunnel or we would have ridden directly into the area of detonation and been tossed into the gorge along with the rest of the detonated material.

By noon we had arrived in Tienhsiang, a little mountain

# THE BUDDHIST NUN AND THE "HOLY FATHER"

village which because of its spectacular scenery had become popular with students and tourists. But this was November and there were none of the summer crowds. The hostel where we would stay was also relatively empty and we were able to get a large room more than big enough for three of us with a well-appointed (western style!) bathroom for the equivalent of $11.00 US.

After lunch we began our climb up the mountain to visit the Buddhist temple. The rain had blown away and the sky was a not unpleasant slate-gray, a perfect temperature for walking – almost cool enough for a sweater. Despite the domestic atmosphere of the hostel and the little shrines and pagodas along the way, this was wild country, the mountains rising starkly arrogant, still untamed. Here was everything I had dreamed about when at Wen Tzao I had sat at my desk correcting mounds of papers, my face and neck and hands wet with perspiration. Then I had longed for mountains – cool, spacious, silent – where I would have time to dream and be free. Yet now that I had it all I found myself apathetic and irritable. All that wonder around me and yet I was unable to open myself to it. Even the road I walked on seemed hostile and I kicked at any pebble that lay in my path.

Part of my reaction was, I realize now as I look back, fatigue. The last four months had drained me – not only the unremitting school work but the strangeness of everything which demanded that I accept, adjust, respond at every minute. This present moment of leisure and freedom had come upon me too suddenly and I closed myself off from it. I was further frustrated by Su-ling and Mei-lan. Despite their adequate command of English, they spoke almost constantly in Mandarin. Occasionally they remembered me and threw a few words in my direction which only intensified my sense of alienation. Happily the steep climb kept conversation to a minimum and when, an hour-and-a-half later, we reached the mountain peak at least part of my irascible temper had been quieted.

The Buddhist temple high upon the mountain was perfectly situated. On two sides it looked down into the valley where the small white houses of Tienhsiang were clustered. Although we had met groups of young people on our climb, the temple precincts themselves were deserted. For a while I stood inside the temple, leaning against a pillar, watching the light of hundreds of candles flicker over the golden face of an immense Buddha. Sticks of incense burned in huge bronze pots but the mountain air kept the sweet smell from being cloying. I stayed a long time, making no active effort to counter my moodiness but simply letting the peace of the mountains and the Buddha seep through my veins.

I had been to only one other Buddhist temple – Fo Kwan Shan, about an hour from Kaohsiung. Fo Kwan Shan was more than a temple, it was a monastery where monks lived in cloister, where they were educated for a life of contemplation. Situated on a large area of level ground everything was cultivated and manicured. Fo Kwan Shan offered a cosmetic landscape, paths and grass groomed, bushes pruned into the shapes of the zodiac. Nothing else I had seen in Taiwan matched its level of perfection.

Buddhism, of course, was not Chinese in origin; it was an imported religion and always in competition with Taoism and Confucianism which were more "native grown." I was fascinated by the fact that no one described these as

# THE BUDDHIST NUN AND THE "HOLY FATHER"

"religions." Taoism, I was told, was simply "The Way," the way to establish peace and harmony as described by Lao Tsu in his *Teh Ching*. Confucianism served the same purpose: to establish right relations so that all could live in harmony. If they were interpreted as religions that was simply the spin Western thought put on them. When I mentioned "God" to my students, they looked at me vaguely as though I were talking of a Western custom like cutting your food with a knife or shaking hands with strangers.

As I watched a cable lifting sacks of rice and a few smaller packages from the valley up to the monastery, a Buddhist nun approached me. She was young, tall, with the high cheek bones of the northern Chinese. She was extraordinarily poised and even with her dull gray tunic and shaven head she was beautiful. It was surprising to find her here in this isolated temple. I was intrigued to discover what had drawn this intelligent young girl not only to the practice of Buddhism but to consecrate her life to it. Since it was soon clear that all her efforts to communicate with me would come to nothing, I motioned her to stay while I went off to find Mei-lan or Su-ling.

For the next hour they sat and talked while I, frustrated, sat listening and understanding nothing.

Here I was in the presence of someone who could tell me of Buddhist life and I was completely closed off. From time to time in response to my persistent questions, Mei-lan offered me a few crumbs but this served only as a further frustration and humiliation. There was an extraordinary quality about this young woman, a sense of peace and inner control. She was obviously bright, curious, sensitive. I wondered what satisfaction "serving the temple" in this remote area could provide. She wanted to talk to us, she explained, because she had heard that there was a "holy father" (a Catholic priest) in the village and she hoped to have an opportunity to talk with him.

It was almost dusk when we started down the mountain road, back to the village: a curious quartet – Su-ling in a grey nun's habit, Mei-lan in a black modified version of the same, our Buddhist in her traditional gray leggings and knee-length tunic, and I – the Westerner – in denim skirt and Aran sweater. On the way we passed some Japanese tourists who stared curiously at us, then covered their mouths, giggling politely.

It had begun to rain by the time we reached the holy father's house – a curious building set on a mountainside just outside Tienhsiang. Father Paul, we later learned, was a Swiss Augustinian priest who, after many years of service, was expelled from Tibet following the Chinese take-over. Like any good Swiss, at home only in the mountains, he had made his way to the inner mountains of Taiwan. Here in this quiet little village he had constructed a Swiss chalet. The effect was startling. The entrance, the house, the gardens all looked like a postcard from Switzerland. To arrive at his residence we climbed a steep flight of brick steps shadowed under a bower of pink and purple blooms. Father Paul had cultivated flowers riotously and created a totally European garden.

Although we were unanticipated visitors he welcomed us graciously into his study. There were books everywhere and in every language: Chinese books, Tibetan books, books in German, French, English. They were piled on the floor, on chairs, on his desk. The walls were covered with travel posters

– all of the country he had left thirty-five years before. Posters of snow-covered mountains, posters of a Swiss chalet, of a man on skis goggled against the blinding snow, of tow-headed children smiling in a lush green meadow – and everywhere pictures of St. Bernard dogs, their mournful eyes staring into the littered room.

Father Paul was tall and angular, a man probably approaching sixty, intense, restless, yet engagingly gentle and attentive to us. His desk was covered with huge bound volumes – his journal kept through the years in exquisite penmanship despite what must have been primitive surroundings. He cleared three chairs of books and pushed aside a mound of photographs, explaining that he was busy writing an account of his most recent trip to Dharamsala, the town on the northern border of India where the Tibetan Government in Exile had been established and where the Dalai Lama had come the preceding summer to visit his exiled people.

It was an arduous trip, he admitted, part of the way by train, then by jeep, finally in a small truck which could negotiate the steep narrow roads and ultimately by foot. He had become sick along the way and had had to rest for several weeks before he could continue. But it was clear that being with the people he loved far outweighed the difficulties. His photographs, which he spread out before us, were startling: the stark, jagged mountains, the grassy plains with their occasional water buffalo, the tents erected to house the thousands of Tibetans who had converged in this isolated spot to hear their spiritual leader once again. To me they were like images of the Old Testament: the strong, lined faces of old men with worn cloaks thrown over their shoulders, young monks, pure and vigilant, in their dark red robes and shaven heads, the women – dark, shy with averted eyes (could those large blue stones which encircled their necks possibly be turquoise?), busy with the primitive business of housekeeping – and the crowds, the vast crowds, close-packed, faces upturned, listening raptly to the Dalai Lama.

For the first time in months communication was no problem for me. Father Paul slipped easily from Taiwanese to Mandarin to French to English. It was blissful to be in the company of someone whose experience and language enabled him to answer my questions. And all the time my eyes strayed to those remarkable photographs which spoke to me of something so mysterious, so transcendent, that by comparison my narrow spirituality seemed bound and withered.

But our visit was ending. Su-ling and Mei-lan were bowing goodbye and our Buddhist nun was arranging to meet the holy father again. As I turned at the doorway for a final thank you, there, silhouetted against the light, were the figures of our Buddhist nun and the Swiss priest and behind them a photograph of a huge St. Bernard, his mournful eyes looking soulfully into the dark.

Before I left I had asked Father Paul if it would be possible to send me copies of some of his photos. Months later, after I had almost forgotten about them, they arrived. I have them still, the colors have faded but the aura remains. I can still conjure up the memory of that mysterious evening and some-times when I am talking to a friend about my years in Taiwan or about those transcendent realities we sometimes lose sight of, I bring them out and go through them one by one. Inevitably the question comes, "What happened to them

# THE BUDDHIST NUN AND THE "HOLY FATHER"

– the priest and the nun?" It comforts me to say, "I don't know." I don't want them in the factual world of questions and answers. They remain for me figures beyond the rational and conceptual. Sometimes I imagine them again: The Nun in her dull gray habit walking down the mountain road into the valley, and the holy father welcoming her in his bright-flowered garden.

ENCOUNTERS

# HOMECOMING

In the summer of 1982 my two years of service in Taiwan were over and in early October I returned to New York. I could hardly have had a more glorious homecoming. Not only did I have joyful friends to welcome me but my novel, *Accidental Grace*, had been published at last. For the next few weeks I was lost in a round of congratulatory events. I was not famous and certainly I was not rich but I was enjoying my own mid-level euphoria. I had written a novel and it had found its way into print! October that year was golden, an unblemished month of dreams fulfilled.

Before leaving Taiwan I had written my letter of resignation from the College of New Rochelle. It was not an easy decision but teaching had never been my first love and my superior, a woman blessed with a genial, laid-back philosophy encouraged my resignation. She did not seem bothered by the loss of income to the community nor by the fact that I had nothing specific planned. She was generous and expansive and encouraged me to "follow my dream." So with some anxiety but with a growing sense of freedom I began to plan my future. With *Accidental Grace* before my eyes I had no doubt that another book was waiting for me. After all I was a published author! What did I have to fear? After so many years of deprivation, so many detours, it seemed that I had brought my life together: I was a nun and I was a "novelist" at last.

It did not take long, however, for *Accidental Grace* to slip into book-oblivion. Even my friends could not be expected to talk about it forever. By the end of the month I was left with nothing else to do but find my way into another book. "Stop worrying; it's too soon," an artist friend cautioned me. She was right, I decided, so I gave myself over to the fine art of dawdling. I spent the mornings enjoying the luxury of several cups of wonderful American coffee while I studied – not just read – *The New York Times*. I rearranged my room. I unpacked books I had stored away. I went shopping, buying new clothes to fit the much thinner person who had returned from two years of rice and fruit. But as October reached into November with darkness closing in earlier each day, my aimless days no longer satisfied me. I heard the ominous words from T.S. Eliot's "Wasteland," "HURRY UP PLEASE IT'S TIME.... HURRY UP PLEASE IT'S TIME."

But time for what? For my next novel, of course. But as I sat in my room with a yellow legal pad on my lap, my mind was blank. "Write what you know about," I had warned my students as they took off in flights of fancy to romantic interludes in Hawaii or the rice paddies of Vietnam. But what did I know about? Suddenly my life seemed very narrow. Most of my adult life had been lived within convent walls. That is what I knew about. I knew about nuns. This was the world I had created successfully in *Accidental Grace*. Surely the world didn't need *Accidental Grace II*. But what else was available to me?

As the days passed with no notes on my yellow pad, I was beginning to lose faith in my imagination. There were, I knew, authors who had produced only a single book; writers who had one story to tell and when they had told it their magic store was exhausted. Was that where I belonged? I had three books behind me but they were biographies not fiction. Was I, after all, not a fiction writer? It was too dark a thought for me to acknowledge.

My room grew daily more oppressive. I needed air and an expanse of sky to free my imagination. Every morning I walked the twenty minutes to Davenport Park, an extensive expanse of grass and trees sloping down to a rockbound inlet of Long Island Sound. It was too late in the season to be popular and ordinarily I had the park to myself. I sat, sometimes for the whole day, watching the tide change and the sun slanting to the west. But when I started home I had nothing to show for it. No notes on paper, no images in my head. I felt like a man who has lost his job but, too ashamed to tell his wife, starts off each morning, briefcase in hand, for his fantasy-job.

Writer's block was a subject I had often discussed with my students. "A generic term," I had explained, covering all kinds of difficulties: fatigue, too much stimulation, not enough fallow time, exerting too much control on material. But was this writer's block? It seemed to me far more deadly. I was losing faith in my imagination; I was losing faith in my "vocation," that inner core of being I had worked so desperately to affirm.

The friendly questions I fielded at dinner came at me

like barbs: "Did you have a good day?" Or worse, "How was your muse today?" Suddenly my life had become a blur of dissatisfaction. All that I had reveled in when I had first come home now seemed foreign; I could not find my place in this world. Back in my own country I felt more isolated than I had in Taiwan. There I was clearly an alien – a Round Eye or Big Nose, as Westerners were often called. Nothing, it was obvious, could ever make me Chinese yet I had never felt excluded. I was alien, yes, but in some way for which I was not responsible. But now I felt alien by design. I had made choices and now I was experiencing their consequences. It was not the first time that the demon of guilt had risen up mocking me for my arrogance in setting myself apart.

It was no help that schools were all in session, that by 8:15 in the morning the convent was practically empty, that dinner conversation centered on new faculty, new students, a promising seminar program. I listened attentively to this language in which I had once participated so easily. What did the Gospel say? "To work I am unable; to beg I am ashamed." Perhaps it was time to be humble. Perhaps it was time to relinquish my writing dreams and look into rejoining the English Department as a humble adjunct.

But one day as I sat on what had become "my bench" at Davenport Park, I watched a boy and his father flying a kite. The giant red and green parrot was caught by the wind and swirled its way up through clouds and into the high blue-sky mountains. The boy's joy was so ecstatic that it carried me with it and later that day as I watched the tide turn and craggy slabs of rock emerge from the water an image began to take shape: a tale of three women.

Imagination had begun to breathe again. In that first catch of joy, without a moment's hesitation, I appropriated Gerard Manley Hopkin's ecstatic line: "The Holy Ghost over the bent/world broods with warm breast and with ah! bright wings." But where Hopkins had written "Holy Ghost," I substituted "imagination." Was that not what imagination was? A sudden movement, divinely given, opening before us what we could never otherwise have discovered? A way God speaks beyond the confines of language and thought? In George Bernard Shaw's "Saint Joan," Joan of Arc, refuting the accusations leveled at her that it was not God who had spoken to her but her imagination, answers: "Of course it is my imagination; how else could God speak to me?" And so, now, as I watched the tide recede and the shadows darken beneath the trees, it seemed that from that most powerful and mysterious abyss God was speaking to me.

Perhaps it was inevitable that the characters that first moved into my consciousness were those of my own family. Although I had no intention of writing an autobiographical novel, I knew that the structure of my family would provide the architecture of the story. It would be a novel of relationships: a father, a mother and two children – the daughter of a first marriage and the unanticipated daughter of a second marriage. It would be a novel of three women: strong-willed, yet insecure, passionately devoted to the husband/father, a man of almost mystical goodness, too innocent to recognize the tangled interaction of the household.

That night my dreams and the little sleepless interludes between were caught up in the bliss of designing a blank canvas. This is the period of "author's delight," the period in which anything is possible. Nothing is beyond reach. The writer has two happy moments, Hemingway is reputed to have said: one before he begins, one after he finishes. In that blissful moment of beginnings, the path seems extraordinarily clear. One has only to order events so that plot, character, setting will converge into a whole. In short, one has nothing to do but "write the book." I was ready. The anxious, exhilarating, expectant months of gestation had begun. And my yellow pad, blank for so long, began to fill.

Soon I was engaged in that biblical act: naming my characters, finding that cryptic combination of letters which, when well chosen, would give these imaginary beings a character and a place. My mind wandered through novels I had loved, reviewing the rightness of the names in Henry James's fiction. I reveled in the rightness of "Charlotte Stant", cool and perceptive, of the sheer Americanism of "Maggie Verver", of the purity and innocence of "Isabel Archer". Their names had caught the essence of their being. I wanted names that would do just that.

Since my novel would revolve around an Irish family I rehearsed all the O'Briens, O'Shaughnessys, O'Maras, O'Connells I could think of but finally decided on the simplicity of Rafferty. The father would be Daniel, a name providing him with a biblical aura. The child of the first marriage would be Bessie, called Elizabeth only on formal occasions. She would be plain, a little dumpy, practical in her interests, a doer. The wife of the second marriage would be a resolute woman, tall, straight, unyielding. She needed a name with hard consonants. She would be Veronica Dorgan. The name for the child of the second marriage was not easy to come by. It must be "special," not taken from the usual category of saints' names – Mary, Kathleen, Ellen – but within the tradition. It must speak of good schools, privilege, manners. Her name would be Natalie.

In the next few weeks with names to guide them, the characters began to identify themselves and the story line began to take shape. Bessie was the youngest of five children, left bereft at the death of their mother. The only girl, with four older brothers, she assuaged her loneliness with her father's love. In the next few years this bond became the center of her life. When he told her of his proposed marriage to Miss Veronica Dorgan, Bessie's favorite teacher, it rose up before her as a terrible act of betrayal not only on her father's part but on the part of her teacher in whom she had confided.

Veronica Dorgan, too, began to develop a life of her own – a life and a character far more complex than that of simply the "second wife." Veronica, competent and independent, was a woman of secrets and silences. I was exhilarated by the possibilities of plot with these two strong-willed women.

It was Natalie who refused to emerge from the shadows. I could find nothing to define her. Her life was uncolored by tragedy or secrets. Unlike Bessie she suffered from no adolescent passions. She was good, compliant, undistinguished. She responded lovingly to her father's affection. She admired and imitated her mother. Although she was uneasy with Bessie's spontaneous candor she felt a secret affection for her. But none of this was enough to win her a place in the company of these two strong and complex women.

While Veronica and Bessie began to weave their relationships, Natalie stood apart, an ill-defined figure who would not emerge from the shadows. I did my best to tease her out. I gave her scenes, events, swatches of dialogue but nothing drew her into the open. If this was writer's reluctance, it was a different kind from any I had ever experienced. For weeks I limped along, irritated and dissatisfied, until one day, with a shock, I recognized my difficulty. Natalie was my *doppelgänger*, my secret self whom I had never acknowledged. She could not emerge from the shadows until I was willing to consent to her reality. It was a moment of chaos, as though, suddenly, without warning, I was faced with the danger of losing my identity. I couldn't explain what was happening but I knew that writing this novel would force me to enter those forbidden spaces, that dark tangle of relations, which I had been taught to skirt and deny. I had not intended to write an autobiographical novel. It was my intention simply to use my family as the basic architecture. Within that structure the characters would be free to develop their personalities and work out the plot lines. But something else had happened.

Stunned and frightened, I ran pell-mell, distancing myself from an enemy who might destroy me. I turned my back on imagination, determined to lose myself in activities which would justify my days. I joined a group of earnest people devoted to the cause of Peace and Justice. I became a member of Literacy Volunteers and struggled each week with a young man whose greatest interest in reading was to enable him to write a love letter to his girl friend and with an old black woman who wanted to be able to read ("not just say") the Our Father before she died. They were people who captured my compassion and together we worked hard to learn how to turn those mysterious black squiggles on a white surface into language.

It took up my days but it did nothing to suppress my

imagination. Natalie was everywhere. She stood before me with her bland smile and her silence. All my efforts to banish her came to nothing. In the end my resistance was broken. I begged her to speak to me. I promised I would listen. I took out the introductory pages of my novel and laid them on my desk. I could not read them at once. I had to feel my way back until I was ready to face that shadowy figure without fear.

"Writing teaches us our mysteries," was a sentence I had read years earlier. It was a thought which had intrigued me. I thought I knew what it meant: that writing was a means for discovering truth, an instrument that forced us to clear the jungle of our thoughts and, as Ezra Pound demanded, set us on a "panther hunt" for the perfect word. But what I was facing now carried that dangerous hunt to a new level.

In the next weeks while snow came and went I sat housebound, listening to Natalie. Sometimes she spoke in rushes, sometimes in short disconnected phrases – sometimes not at all. Even in her long silences I knew I could do nothing else but wait for her. I waited while her labored images colored my imagination and drew me into her consciousness. She pulled me relentlessly below the surface of this quiet family to where the unacknowledged tensions lay.

I saw Bessie, beloved child of the first marriage, fighting to keep her place, as she watched Veronica not only replace her mother but take Bessie's own place in her father's heart. And I saw Veronica, so confident, so assured, using her imperious manner to hide the fear and resentment of knowing she could never be Daniel's first love. Natalie, silent, had absorbed it all. It had shaped her. Long before she was old enough to understand the dynamic she suffered its consequences. She knew that leaning to either one side or the other would be regarded as a treacherous act. She must be careful in everything.

Unequal to the role in which she felt herself cast, she withdrew. Below the surface the rumblings of the earth's plates continued but she had learned to create her own world, a world of the imagination where she found shelter. She smiled and was silent, distancing herself from the tensions around her. Silence became her safe-house, her refuge.

This was the Natalie I had begged to speak to me, the Natalie I listened to, as she uncovered a self I had refused to acknowledge. Little by little I was learning to accept this new awareness as the last snows melted and the dark days of Lent led us on toward Easter.

*Solo Voices*, my novel would be called. The melody, the harmony, the counterpoint of three women in their tangled love cycle. Veronica, Bessie, Natalie. So far I had caught only a confused triad of voices. How the voices would mesh and interpret each other was still beyond me but I had a focus for my novel and I was beginning to hear three distinctive voices For the rest I would trust myself to my mantra: "Writing teaches us our mysteries."

It was still a long time till spring but the mornings were brighter now and when it snowed, the flakes on the sidewalks melted as soon as they fell. It was time, I knew, to begin my novel.

# ENCOUNTERS

Coda:

*Some two years later Solo Voices was a finished manuscript. Of course I was not "satisfied"; what author ever is? But when I handed it to my agent I was "pleased." She called me a week later – record time to get the assessment of an agent. She loved Solo Voices and predicted that she would be able to sell it in record time.*

*Alas, she was wrong. After some eighteen anxious months, I had a hefty file of rejections, all of them saying relatively the same thing: This engaging novel is not right for our list at this time.*

*It was a decision not easy to accept. Perhaps it is true, as some authors assert, that it is the book which costs us the most that we love the most. Even today, decades later, I take out Solo Voices (still in manuscript) and read through the chapters with affection and regret. I love these people, these three women I came to know so well. As for my initial fear of "losing my identity" – quite the opposite happened. It was when the self from which I had hidden for so long began to emerge that I found my voice.*

*Writing teaches us our mysteries.*

ENCOUNTERS

# NOVA NADA JOURNAL

*Nova Nada is a small "solitude community" situated in the wilderness of eastern Nova Scotia. It is not hard to establish solitude here for it is in every way "out of the swing of the sea," inaccessible to the casual traveler.*

*One turns inland from Yarmouth, traveling along narrow country roads, passing an occasional house built far back from the "highway." The last six miles are covered on a dirt road, fairly smooth in summer and early fall, snow-covered in winter, and a lake of mud in the spring thaw. At the final approach there is a gate across the road and a wooden sign: "Be still and see that I am God."*

*Beyond the gate is Nova Nada: a series of small wooden hermitages where in addition to the small permanent community guests may come to visit for a few days or stay on for a few months. It is a place of steady, unbroken quiet and great beauty. The lake around which the hermitages are built is long and transparently clear. It is, in fact, the first in a series of lakes, a never-ending waterway leading deep into the interior. The forest is still virgin, thick with conifers, maples, birches. Such "essentials" as heat, light, water are of necessity primitive.*

*I am not sure when I first heard of Nova Nada, even less sure when I decided that I must go there. I was longing for a desert experience although I was far from understanding what this would be. I had no definite plan in mind. I knew only that I needed to walk away from the familiar, to search for God in a place where there was nothing else to find. I needed to find The Unknown in order to face the unknown in myself. It was a time in my life shaped by the changes of Vatican II. In many ways it was a successful period in my life. My teaching, my lecturing, my writing were enough to satisfy my ego but there was another part of me which was dry and empty. Repeatedly, into the bustle of living, came Jung's insistent injunction: Our first obedience must be to our intuition. Whatever else I was obeying I knew I was not obeying my intuition: to give in to my insistent hunger for a wilderness solitude.*

*For two years allusions to Nova Nada bombarded me from all sides. It was like a new word that once noticed seems to crop up everywhere. When, ultimately, I wrote asking if I might have a hermitage for a month or so it was less a decision than a surrender. I was going to be obedient to my intuition at last.*

*The last lap of my journey to Nova Nada was made in the pickup truck of an elderly gentleman – eighty-two on his next birthday, he told me proudly. When he learned that there was a visitor going to Nova Nada, he graciously offered transportation. "I take you d'ere," he volunteered in his unique French-Canadian accent, assuring me that he knew the way, that he sometimes drove out on a Sunday to visit. "I go to take a look," he explained. "I never stay in d'at place. D'at some place d'at!"*

*I could only nod. Now that I was actually on my way terror had begun to creep up over my ankles. My friend was not given to hyperbole. He had already told me that he had been a lumberman for years, had led hunting expeditions, had been lost for three days in a blizzard and even now walked five miles every day to keep in trim. If he said that Nova Nada was "some place," then it must be indeed.*

*"You like d'e woods?" he asked. I thought of the well-peopled trails and paths around Bear Mountain in eastern New York, my deepest woodland experience, and nodded.*

*"All woods d'ere," he explained, pointing his chin toward the road ahead. "And lakes. Nova Scotia, she got lots lakes. You look down from de aeroplane, you see all water." That was nice to know, I said. The paved road had ended and we were bouncing along a narrow dirt road.*

*"You see d'at house in d'ere?" he asked, pointing to a little cabin. "I live d'ere once. My son, he come to see me one day. He say, 'Papa, I bring you a radio. It's nice you listen in d'e evening.' So I listen but d'en I see d'e deer not come close no more. D'at radio, she scare off my deer. So I t'rew d'at damn t'ing out." For a moment he relived his victory over technology and gave me a tight triumphant smile.*

*As we drove further into the wilderness I would have bolted without him. Terror was creeping up fast. But he gave me no chance to change my mind. He told me with pride and awe of the snow, the cold, the early winters and late thaws. He told me there was no electricity but that there was a fine well where I would get my water. Good, clean water. He shook his head in admiration of such a life. "D'ey pray all d'e time, d'eese people."*

*A half-hour later he left me at the main gate, my suitcase with its protective straps and identification tag looking foolishly urbane on the dirt path.*

*September 1*

I have never written by lamplight before. Less steady, less bright, less predictable than the bulb I have always taken for granted. Strange and a little eerie – but beautiful in its own way. Those giant shadows looming over the page do not make it easy. I think from now on I will keep my diary during daylight hours.

*September 2*

So at last I am here. There are seven people presently in residence at Nova Nada: four of the permanent staff (2 priests, a young seminarian, a Sister administrator) and three of us guests seeking solitude in our various ways. In addition to the hermitages there is a small simple chapel and a main house where, I gather, we will occasionally share a communal meal.

All my decisions, made and remade, my meticulous planning – even my final terrors – are behind me. The last I left somewhere on the road – not, indeed, replaced by courage but by a kind of numbness. I have entered such an unknown land that my ordinary emotions are useless. After so many weeks of intense feeling, feelings no longer work. Having arrived at my goal at last, I find myself lost.

I am wary in this strange environment – wary and hostile. I must be on guard, alert to protect myself from what is alien and dangerous. But why am I surprised? I have grown up in cities where the environment very often **is** hostile. You'd have to be pretty crazy not to keep your house locked, your apartment bolted, your car alarmed, your bicycle chained. You learn to hold firmly to your pocketbook, to keep the flap inside close to your body, not to use deserted subway stations.

So, of course, you have learned to be always "on guard."

It is not an attitude that is cast off lightly. Although I know there is small chance of intruders in this distant place, my body says, "Careful now; be alert . . . you never can tell." Surely there must be spiritual implications of such a stance. If even the "known" can be so dangerous, then what of the great unknown mysterious God? The force that controls, the Invisible One? We have been told that he is kind, good, beneficent. "Faith" tells us so but having been taught since childhood not to talk to strangers what enormous barriers there must be in us to trust the greatest Stranger of all.

*September 4*

This is an awesomely beautiful place. Pines so tall there seem no end to them – lacy, feathery pines. And birches: some old, gnarled, gray, fuzzy – until you look up and see the white glory at the top. The sky was blue today and the lake sapphire and filled with fire-points. This evening, sitting in the dark by the lake, wrapped in my poncho with my hands in borrowed gloves (kindly lent since I had not thought to bring any – after all, it is still summer) I watched those giant trees reflected in the black water. Then, with the afterglow, the reflections turned pink, mauve, lavender, smudged a little by an evening breeze until it all looked like a scene from a giant Japanese vase. I stayed long after I was chilled through. It seemed somehow "unmannerly" to leave, like walking out in the midst of a symphony.

*September 5*

There is singing in the forests today, a kind of susurration. "Drop down dew, ye heavens," the psalmist begged and as I listen the rain comes to earth. As I watch it out my window I feel watered by infinite kindness, washing away the soil of my fears. There is peace here, and love, and something I do not understand. The understandable I have left behind. And here in the unknown I begin to discover an unknown self. There is nothing here for me to hold on to, nothing that identifies me. Is this how I shall discover God, a God who is at once nothing and everything? Even this is beyond my understanding. I must be content for a while with unknowing. Beyond my window the pine trees lift themselves to the rain, growing heavy but unbowed.

*September 7*

I slip to the edge of the black creek at the foot of my hermitage and fill my pail with water for elemental needs. Then on to the well to pull up water to drink. This lucid water: clarity, wisdom, purity. Water that is "nothing." *Nada – speculum sine macula.* Water without speck or stain.

Then back up the path, slippery with pine needles and black earth. My poncho beaded with rain and my sneakers sodden. I am wet and cold and yet it does not matter because I am overwhelmed in the music of the rain. The birds are silent – smart enough to rest in this music. Perhaps, too, I will learn to rest and be still.

Then through my routine domestic thoughts, God makes his way, nudging me, like a distraction, to be with him.

*September 10*

Stumbling out of bed – truly stumbling because it is dark beyond any darkness I have ever known. The prayer-bell down by "Elias" clangs through the forest – through sleep – through cold. Then the panther hunt for the matches. Think. Think. Where did you leave them last night? When will you remember to leave them near the lamp! Then cold fingers finding them. One goes out, another. I feel only three more in the box. Not room for too many more mistakes. Then, finally, one stays and I grope to turn the wick up on the lamp, fumbling ineptly. Then at last: the flare of light.

Dressing is elemental. All my clothes so insufferably warm yesterday under the garden sun are now like gossamer. I plunge the plastic cup into the bucket of well water. Almost empty now – but just enough if you tip it carefully. Face washed, teeth brushed, lamp blown out – carefully, carefully. And out into the dark.

The small well of light cast by my flashlight points at the path, slippery with night dew and the treachery of half-covered roots.

I pause to look at the lake – immense and forbidding – through the trees. The stars are gone and the first sullen gray just beginning. The time for questions, for doubts. "Shall these bones live?" I ask. But I am no longer remembering Ezechiel from thousands of years ago; I am no longer quoting Eliot, poet to poet. This is my question now. I ask it, not out of memory, not out of rhetoric, but as one asks who does not know.

What shall live today? The world seems as tenuous as the blurred outline of the lake. What shall live? Is the world, so substantial, so self-sufficient, so full of business and bombs and jet planes, is it no more substantial than the mists of the lake? Reality? I have no answer.

What shall this day be?

A day of light? A day of rain?

A day of growing or of destruction?

Perhaps to the experienced, the nature-wise, it is all clear. But I know nothing in this foreign place. Shall I live this day in your light, my God? I know now a little of what that means. With only my kerosene lamp to push the darkness back, I know now that light is everything. The sun is light, heat, power. "O Oriens," we used to sing in Advent. "Come, Lord Jesus." Now in this place all my nights are Advent – dark, unknown, yearning for light. And in the pre-dawn I pray, O Oriens, that you will rise upon us, your sunlight dispelling the darkness of night presences, those phantoms that crowd about me in the dark. Come upon us, Sun of Justice. Calm our fear. Give light to the blind, as you have promised. Give us your light that we may see Light.

*September 11*

Sunlight through the trees as I walk to the well. Then for a moment I stand motionless at the lake's edge. One drop of dew on a woodbine leaf: shining cold diamond, then yellow fire, then turning to flame, brighter than flame but steady, poised, sure, receiving sunlight, turning from water to pure light. Then for a moment yellow fire again, then diamond – then gone. And another dewdrop higher up – finding light on a far-finger of a barberry bush.

Then back to the well, heady with light, to my bucket. I am more skilful now, able to send down the bucket sideways so the water slips across the lip and sinks the pail to fill it.

Then up, hand over hand, the pulley turning.

"I am the living water" – and my pail is full.

*September 15*

Harvest time although it is only mid-September. The first frosts will come soon and there are rows and rows of vegetables to harvest. I worked in the garden this afternoon. It is a good place to be. Alone. Quiet. Beets are easy to harvest. You can see them rising out of the soil. One pull and they are yours. Ready, glad to come. Beans are less compliant. The plants grow low and tangled and the beans themselves (camouflaged because they are the same color as their leaves) are irritatingly hidden. No way to do this but on your knees, plant by plant. Slow work in which there are few comfortable positions.

I think of the migrant workers who do this for life. Always stooping, bent over, the strong sun scorching the back of your neck. I am here hardly more than an hour and it is already enough. A life like this? Anxious, harassed, paid by the basket. No joy in the harvest. They did not plant these seeds or tend these plants. This harvest is not theirs. It is not mine either but there is some joy in sharing this labor – some joy in heaping the basket, in doing the elemental task man has always been engaged in – gathering food that he may live. So little of my life is simple that I revel in this slow, solitary labor that leaves my mind free. And I find you here camouflaged among the beans, my God, and know you a little better as Creator.

*September 17*

A strange day: "Visiting Sunday." It happens once a month

when Nova Nada opens its gates and says to the surrounding countryside: "Come and see." Most of the people who wander in are from around Yarmouth and vicinity. They are simple, country people, with little to say. Mostly they stare, say a few awkward words in French-Canadian accents, and depart – convinced, I suppose, that they have seen "a hermit" – the next best thing to having seen a ghost!

I was rather unprepared for all this and was sitting at my table by the window when I felt a shadow. I looked up and there were two ladies and a bearded gentleman, peering in, hands cupped at the sides of their heads the better to see. The window was closed but I bowed a little and made a peace sign; they made no response but stared a bit longer and then walked on. I suppose I should have thought of some hermit-like thing to do. I think I was rather a disappointment.

Later I had moved to my doorway to catch a little sun when I noticed a strange crunching, clawing sound. I looked up and only about twenty feet away I saw a grotesque animal about the size of a medium-sized dog. He was awkwardly, laboriously inching his way up a large birch tree. It was obviously an effort for him. He looked rather like a fat lady puffing up the subway stairs with heavy shopping bags. He was brown-gray, short-legged and heavy-haired. Beyond that I could not see. From the safety of my doorway it was fascinating to watch his ponderous ascent.

At precisely that moment came a Sunday family: mother, father, and rambunctious child scuffing through the leaves, pulling on the branches and – all unknown – heading for my mysterious animal who was now about ten feet off the ground. "Hello," I said, searching for a tone which would warn them without frightening them. "Listen, I don't think he better go over there; I think there's a bear climbing the tree." This was more than enough for Maman who screamed, "Robert," pulling her son back against the cabin and glaring at me as though I had deliberately sent him into this perilous trap.

Papa was calmer. "Where is your bear?" he asked. I didn't argue over the possessive adjective but pointed toward the tree. "Ah," he said, shaking his head. "He is no bear. This is porcupine. Very big. Usually comes smaller," he concluded, shaping his hands to suggest a large cat. I nodded but could think of nothing to say. Changing the bear to a porcupine did not essentially reassure me. Mother swept me once more with an angry look and marched Junior ahead of her down the path. Just once she turned. "You live here?" she asked. I nodded, overwhelmed by the fact that for the time being I do.

*September 20*

Surely it is fitting (considering my temperament) that of all the creatures in this woodland paradise it should be a porcupine who has taken up residence in my "backyard." Although I have not known him long, I have assumed a rather proprietary air (almost maternal) toward Porqui. Such are the hazards of solitude. The night of the electric storm when I crouched in my cabin in terror, I kept wondering about Porqui. Does he hide? Is there an underground place for him to go to? Does the rain seep through all those quills? And is he, underneath that fearful hide, really afraid? I discovered him the next morning, sodden but unmoving, in the top crotch of a birch tree which seems to be his permanent residence.

He is tragi-comedy at its best, the kind of ugliness that will always provoke laughter. He is neither sinister nor evil. There is nothing quick or clever or sharp about him – except that body-quiver of quills and even they seem an ugly burden to him. He is, I have observed, a leaf-and-bark eater and a tree dweller. One of the high-rise people of the forest. But at what cost! The slow, ponderous body with its tiny head, its short thin legs, inching upward. His quills extend only half-way down his back, leaving the great ugly black rump unprotected. The tiny forelegs reach up, clutch the bark and tug. The rear legs inch out, reach up in their turn and the graceless body drags itself upward a foot or so.

What, I wonder, does Porqui think as those quick, brown squirrels with their rickety, clicking sounds run up and down the trees beside him. Brilliantly quick, graceful, gay with companionship, the squirrels have it all! Old Porqui is so alone, so ugly, so brute. Poor Caliban. But then my fairy-tale mind begins to imagine: perhaps he is really a handsome prince under the spell of an evil sorcerer! I like that. It will console me for a while.

*September 22*

Yesterday was a day made by the gods for the gods. After three cold, foggy days, it came to me like Eden. The sun was high and warm, the sky cloudless blue and the lake without a ripple.

I took the canoe – the big one named Gandhi. It doesn't respond as easily as Nikos but it has better balance and a place to put my books. I paddled to the end of the first lake and around the little island. This is as far as I'd ever gone because usually the wind hits you here and I'm not strong enough (or brave enough) to right the canoe. But this morning not a single breath of wind. I paddle on, the reflections of the trees in the water so perfect that I feel as though I were engaged in some mystic passage, gliding along tree tops and through the boughs of giant pines which blur and crumple and dissolve as my paddle cuts through the water. Two worlds merging. One, the hard cold wood and water world of canoe and lake which must be minded carefully or I will go overboard with some heedless motion or hit a rock or catch on a sandy reef hidden just below the water-lily pads. The other world: the world of reflection, of imagination, just as real and just as dangerous. This world casts a spell. You drift on, unaware of how far you have gone, lost in a world where it seems you are limitlessly free, unaware that you have been enthralled. Now suddenly I dip my paddle, narrowly avoiding a rock – and return to the world of dark water and hard wood.

I have gone far, far beyond the first lake. I am in a new place, a place I have never been before. Still no wind. The world of reflection is still perfect. I pull out further into the lake to feel the full freedom of gliding through tree tops. The sun is hotter here and I pull off my sweater – carefully, carefully, with great respect for the delicate balance of Gandhi.

Then as suddenly and as clearly as a drop of water falling from the paddle onto my wrist, God's presence touches me. "Thou," I say and close my eyes. In a little while I beach the canoe on a sandy strip of shore. I put my sweater over a rock and lean against it in that silence I can never create but only respond to.

He is everything. I have said it for so long and learn it

a little day by day. He is the mystic point where my worlds meet. He is my experience and because he is my experience he is for me the Great Undeniable. In affirming him I affirm all that I experience. No need to unravel the distinctions between reality and reflection, shadow and substance.

"You are the world and its fullness," the psalmist sings. Yes, I believe it. Word-Builder, Mountain-Wielder, Ocean-Shaper. You ARE.

Yet out of the vastness of his creation, out of the immensity of his being, comes the slow-spoken gentleness of his presence to create me, to create the uncreate-able in me. To touch and quicken what had not existed. The worlds in me – so often disparate and warring – slip into harmony. I live. Thou.

*September 23*

I returned this morning to my little patch of beach, hoping to find, I suppose, what had awaited me yesterday. The cove was empty and I was left with only "remembrances of things past." It was very warm and I thought lazily of going swimming. Instead I lay on the beach and dozed. Suddenly I was startled awake by a great thrashing in the underbrush. Panic! Until Ish, tail beating wildly, came leaping toward me. He had followed me through the woods and was irrepressibly delighted that he had caught up with me at last. I was licked thoroughly and then we sat together looking out over the water. He is a beautiful little Border Collie, indistinguishable from his brother except for a wider stripe down his nose and a more adventuresome spirit.

Suddenly Ish was on his feet growling before I sensed

anything. Then out of the trees on the far side of the lake flew a large awkward bird, coming to rest quite near us on the lake. Ish was beside himself. He dashed for the water but when he was in a few feet he drew back – too fastidious (or too frightened) to go on. Then the bird rose a little and gave that strange, eerie, quavering loon cry. Almost immediately from the same corner of the woods came a second loon, lighting beside the first. They swam together in small circles, side by side but facing in opposite directions. Ish (smart dog) recognizing the unobtainable had stopped barking and was watching motionless in the grasses at the lake's edge. The birds let themselves be carried by the current and soon they were too far away to be seen distinctly. They seemed to be bending over each other, one of them preening and lifting its long neck out of the water. Then their necks crossed and they were still. A mating ritual? Hardly in September. More probably a lice-picking party – less romantic but closer to the truth.

Far off I could distinguish the rhythmic beat of a canoe expertly paddled – someone from Nova Nada in Nikos. Although I strained to see I could catch only a small dark speck in the distance.

*September 26*

I must have side-stepped at least eight snakes on my way to the well this morning. They seem a little groggy – maybe still besotted from the tons of rain that fell on us last night. The toads are hopping too – quite openly, not even keeping to the grass. "Careful of those snakes," I warn them, picking a sleepy one from the side of a puddle. He is pretty: brown and gray-speckled. He blinks but is otherwise unresponsive. I throw him into the grass, momentarily out of harm's way.

*September 28*

This morning the well is half-sunlight, half-shade. I let my bucket down and bring it up carelessly, lulled by my growing expertise. It lurches unexpectedly against the stones and in a flash my white plastic pail which I had rested precariously on the rim is over the top and into the well. I lunge after it but I'm too slow. I can see it quite distinctly, floating on its side, drawing water very slowly. It will be a long time before it completely sinks.

Suddenly my imagination, all unbidden, recalls medieval tales of the "oubliettes," those places of silent torture – the "forgotten place," where the victim was thrust down below the earth, then fed just enough to keep him alive in his dark solitude. "A man forgotten and without hope." The edge of madness. The psalms I had so often read unreflectively now swirl around me: "Lord, I cry to you at break of day; I cry to thee, my God, why have you forgotten me; hear my cry, O God, in my despair I call to you." And that bleakest and loneliest of all cries, the cry of Christ dying in his own oubliette – "My God, My God, why have you forsaken me?"

Behind me Father Michael comes to fill his pail. I cannot raise my eyes from the dark water. "Somethin' wrong?" he asks, his Utah "r" lingering in the air. "Down there," I say pointing. "Down there. I lost my pail."

*October 1*

Last night I sat looking into the woods, doing nothing but watching the light fade in the forest. But to do that, I have found, is to do everything, to engage one's whole attention, to center one's whole being on the cosmic/personal, awesome/tender fading of the light. It is to die. To say goodbye. This day is over. I cannot hold it back, recast it, change the script. It is not mine. It was a gift. My regret is not to have received it more attentively, not to have cherished it, not to have given myself to it more lovingly, more completely. "Into your hands I commend myself." I have said it a thousand times and known so seldom what I was saying.

But now as the light between the trees darkens and the trees themselves merge – the white birches last – I know that with this day I die into your hands. In this alien place I have little that I think of as "my life." My work, my friends, my books, my music, my clothes – all these I have left behind that I might enter your presence, my God, less encumbered, more purely. Now, at nightfall, you ask me to sacrifice one more thing: the light of day and the day itself. Little by little you withdraw them from me and I watch them go until only the blurred outline of a dying pine remains.

It has been a gentle night-fall. You have taken the day quietly; now there is only one more thing for me to do. I finger my regrets. They are all that is left of the day: my impatience so quick and so unmerited; my petulance before the unanticipated; my wariness which makes me circle suspiciously like a dog around the love you offer me. Most of all my fears. And now I gather them all in the palms of my hands, like wounds I hold out to you for you to heal. I close my eyes. Into thy hands, O Lord.

*October 4*

I am coming to the end of my solitude experience. What

has happened to me in these days, in this place? Yesterday as I sat in the sunlight, leaning my feet against a rock jutting into the lake I found myself still wary and reluctant to accept the reaches of solitude. For me, bred in cities of one kind or another, it was simply too much. Not frightening in any ordinary sense of the word, as one might fear to be raped or mugged in a lonely place. It was not fear I felt but wonder, awe, a shaking of my universe and of my place in it. I was balancing precariously on the cliff's edge where I must redefine myself in a reality totally different from anything I could have conceived. I have begun to sense in my aloneness the total, overarching, inescapable sweep of the cosmic God.

"Wherever I go, you are there," the psalmist wrote. It is true but not in the narrow sense I had imagined. He is there because He Is. He is all. The Other. There is nothing else because there is nothing else. The wonder is not that He is but that I am. I am the accidental one, the dispensable one. But drunk with my own being – and surrounded by other inebriates – I can only be brought to this cold, sober truth in solitude. I have begun to discover that when all those things that pamper my vision of my reality slip away, I, too, disappear a little. The artificial distinctions set up to categorize and make things manageable slip away. And the world is truly God's and I am God's, not through some feeble, halting act of my will but in the immense fiat of creation.

Those household gods, those kindly beings who kept me safe when I offered them scraps from my table, are gone. I must serve a new God, the God who declared, "I am who am, the first and the last, the beginning and the end." The old myth that I have only to turn in his direction to eliminate the distance between us now seems meaningless. The distance between us is immense, truly an abyss which no human desire can bridge. He is. He is the Other. And yet because He is, He is also the sustaining power of my being. He is with me innermostly. I am with Him because He is all. While I cannot bridge the abyss that separates us, yet neither can I be apart from Him. He is Everything and Nothing. This is the experience of my solitude.

Instead of arguing with the paradox, I let it seep through me like light.

In this light, I see
What I see is Light itself.
The Light is a single Word.

I will not cut the diamond; the stone is too precious.

ENCOUNTERS

# SEEING IN THE DARK

On an early spring morning I had walked up to the college chapel to attend the morning liturgy. Along the way I counted five crocuses: three yellow and two a mixture of purple and white. I waved to Lenny, our gardener, who was planting pansies in the urns in front of the Castle. I liked this morning service which routed me out early and got me to my office shortly after nine. I was presently concluding research for the book which would become *Lady Blackrobes*. The hours of reading microfilm and interpreting handwritten texts were almost complete and now I was looking forward to the exciting (and perilous) process of putting all the diverse material in order.

The service proceeded with its usual quiet until the prayers of the offertory, when, without warning, I experienced silent explosions of light in my left eye. For a moment I was dazzled but before I had time to realize what was happening, it was over.

Around me the congregants were responding to the "Sanctus" and I stood with them. Mass continued. At first I thought the flashes of light had something to do with the electric system. The chapel roof was being repaired at the time and we were surrounded by leaning beams and dangling wires. But the lights were still functioning and no one else seemed to have shared my experience. It was, I realized, not the electrical system but my eye that had exploded. I blinked and looked around. Everything seemed normal; my vision had not changed. When it was time to receive communion, I joined the communicants, walking without difficulty to receive the host.

When Mass was over I put on my coat and started for my office. Along the way I kept opening and closing my eyes alternately to see if my left eye was still functioning. No problem. I went to my office and got to work. I continued to work until lunch. I thought once or twice of calling my ophthalmologist but there didn't seem to be anything worth saying since the experience was so quickly over and had seemed to have had no permanent consequences.

Was it a week later – maybe more – that I woke up one night and turned to look at my clock. In place of the clock face which usually blazed at me, I could see nothing but a faint glimmer of light. I blinked but nothing changed. I tried again. Nothing. It took me a while to realize that my hand was covering my right eye. I lowered it and blinked again and there was my clock as bright as ever. Clearly it was only my left eye which was affected. For the next half hour I experimented, covering my left eye, then my right, staring at the clock, turning on the light over my bed and focusing on different objects in my room. The framed image of Fra Angelico's Annunciation, the lines of calligraphy from Gerard Manley Hopkins' poem, "Margaret are you grieving," the small porcelain statue of the Chinese fisherman – they were all there, true and clear, as long as I kept my right eye uncovered. When I used only my left eye they disappeared, leaving only a peripheral ring of light around them. It was 2:30 a.m.

I turned off the light and lay on my back, the covers drawn up to my chin. For a while I continued the game of left eye, right eye. For the first time I acknowledged that those momentary explosions which I had dismissed so cavalierly did, in fact, have consequences. After a while I fell asleep, taking comfort in the hope that by morning my world would right itself again.

But the morning changed nothing. Before noon I was in my ophthalmologist's office waiting for a verdict. Dr. Klamen had treated me for years and was now on the verge of retirement. We went through the usual eye examination procedures but it was immediately clear that I could see almost nothing with my left eye. He sat silent for a few minutes and then asked, "Do you have headaches?" No, not often. "Have you noticed memory loss?" Not really. He sighed and turned away. "I can't be sure that this is an eye problem. Perhaps you should have a brain scan," he suggested. The words paralyzed me. "Just a precaution," he assured me. "There are more sophisticated eye tests than I am equipped to do." He reached for his rolodex and began flipping through the cards. "I'm going to make an appointment for you with an excellent retinologist," he continued. "He has an office in Port Chester; can you go this afternoon?" I nodded but questioned, "Can he see me at such short notice?" My experience with eye doctors was weeks (or months) of waiting before you could get an appointment. He nodded, picking up the phone, "This is an emergency."

By mid-afternoon I sat listening to a retinologist explain to me the causes and consequences of macular degeneration. Or AMD (age-related macular degeneration) as he familiarly referred to it. AMD was of two major types: dry and wet. Dry was the most common, affecting over 85% of those suffering from the disease. It was, at the beginning, hardly noticeable and progressed very slowly. It was often years before the disease led to partial blindness. The less common form was wet AMD. Far less common, it was more dramatic in its approach, often manifesting itself suddenly and with rapid development.

The tests he would conduct, with my permission, would determine definitively which form of AMD I was suffering from and what damage I had already incurred. He seemed to have little doubt that I was a victim of wet AMD but fluorescent angiography would provide a definitive diagnosis. An hour later I had the result: I was suffering from neovascular degeneration. New blood vessels grow beneath the retina and leak blood. The leakage causes permanent damage to light-sensitive cells which die off, creating blind spots in the central vision.

"When did these explosions happen?" the doctor asked. "Maybe about a week ago," I said.

"And before that," he asked, "did you notice difficulty seeing?"

"No, nothing. I had cataract surgery but that wasn't a problem. My eyes were fine until I had these explosions of light in my left eye. Is that the way it usually happens?"

He shook his head, frowning. "Rarely," he answered.

"Most people don't get such a dramatic wake-up call. What did you do?"

"Nothing." I stumbled, trying to explain my reaction.

He looked at me quizzically. "You must have known something was wrong. You didn't see your ophthalmologist?"

I was blushing with embarrassment. In retrospect my failure to act made me feel like an idiot. "It didn't bother me; I could still see," I explained.

He nodded, studying the computer screen which displayed the results of the angiography: the retina and the surrounding area of my eye enlarged in beautiful color. Had I seen him immediately, he explained, there might have been a chance of saving my vision, but I had waited too long. I had missed my wake-up call. But, he assured me, he could offer me some good news. Great progress was being made in the treatment of macular degeneration. There was a new procedure which in most cases would halt the progress of the condition. The bad news was that in a significant number of people the second eye would also become affected.

Of all the medical terminology I heard that afternoon, the only word that pulsed in my head as we drove home was "irreversible." I had suffered an irreversible loss of vision.

In the next few months I underwent the recommended procedures and had regular appointments with my retinologist who assured me that things were going well. Although there was no possibility of regaining my sight the hope was to stabilize my eye so that no further loss would occur. During those weeks I acquired a new vocabulary. There was exudative and non-exudative AMD. There was drusen, choroid, retinal pigment. I learned that smoking, obesity, heredity, even race can be a factor in this pervasive condition. I can't recapture the tenor of those days except to say that I was obsessed with seeing. Was I seeing more or less, was the print in *The New York Times* lighter today than it had been yesterday? The left eye/right eye test seldom left me. I tried it on trees as I walked to my office, I walked with my head down examining the bluestone slabs on the campus paths. I looked in the mirror studying to find some difference in the way my eyes looked.

And my head teemed with images of light. Had the poetry I had taught for so long always been so permeated with references to light? Why had I been so insensible to them? But that had been in a time I could hardly recapture, a time when "seeing" was taken for granted as the ordinary way of life. "I wake and feel the fell of dark not day," my beloved Hopkins had written in his effort to convey the anguish of depression. "Go not gentle into that dark night/But rage, rage against the dying of the light." But Dylan Thomas's fury was not for me. I was not raging, I was suppliant before the threat of darkness. Was it Henry Vaughan who had given me that wondrous image of heaven, "I saw eternity the other night/Like a great ring of pure and endless light"? But it was not eternity I longed to see but the domestic realities of my daily life.

My concern now was for what I had come to call "my good eye." The diminishment of the other one I was learning to accept. I knew the meaning of "irreversible." Although I lived with the possibility of partial blindness, I was comforted by the assurance that I would never completely lose my peripheral vision. But such comfort did little to rescue me from anxiety. I lived each day in a foreign country where I did not know the language or the customs. I could only wait to learn the extent of my exile.

By the following spring I had "good news." The vessels in my left eye were no longer leaking; my eye had stabilized. My right eye, although prone to dry macular degeneration, showed no signs of neovascular degeneration. As my retinologist continued to monitor my condition, he assured me that he expected no further dramatic changes. Although the process of dry macular degeneration would continue in my right eye, it would be a slow process; not something for immediate worry. It was now simply a question of learning to live with diminished vision.

Surely there was irony in the fact that I whose life had been a matter of reading and writing should be so afflicted. I could never remember a time when reading was not only my most successful escape but my greatest joy. As the single child of older parents, I had early on learned to be self-sufficient and self-contained. Books were my teachers, my friends, my magic island. In time they became my profession and remained my joy.

What now was being asked of me? I acknowledged that I had been blessed beyond my prayers. I was far from blind and . . . and yet. The research which I had always loved had become a frustrating experience. I came home from my office exhausted, only to find that reading, the escape which had always solaced me, was now beyond my reach.

Of course there were supports. Through The Lighthouse, that extraordinary organization which provides help for the visually challenged, I was able to get tapes from the vast storehouse provided free of charge. It was a wealth beyond my imagining. It seemed there was nothing I could ask for that they could not provide. But even with all this wealth available I found myself petulant, longing for a book, a book to hold, a book with pages to turn, enabling me to go back and reread a paragraph which intrigued me. Rewinding a tape and getting to the exact paragraph I wanted required a patience I did not have. Listening, I was discovering, was not quite the same as reading. It needed a skill I had not yet developed.

But I was too obstinate to give in easily. Again and again I pushed aside the tapes in favor of a book even though I knew that I could not sustain reading for more than a short period. After a little while the type lost its clarity and I was left trying to see through a blur. I used eye drops more frequently; I tried to remember to blink, as I had been instructed. For a minute or so the blur would clear – but never for long.

Was this to be my new country? Not the bleak, dramatic country of the blind but simply the Land of Blur. It could hardly have been a land more antithetical to my training and my psychology. I had a passion for clarity. Clarity for me was more than clear thought. It was a word I impregnated with the values I loved most. Clarity was truth; it was light. It was what brought meaning out of chaos. *Claritas*, if I remembered correctly, was a word that Thomas Aquinas predicated of beauty.

As a teacher I had had no tolerance for the lazy, inexact sentence. "Fuzzy" I wrote in the margins of dozens of papers. I wanted language to be hard and exact. I demanded that my students be ruthless in their search for the precise word, that they hone their sentences to rigorous precision. Fuzzy would not do.

*Claritas*, I was beginning to understand, had ruled not only my teaching but my spirituality. Along with its cognate, "truth," I pursued it with passion – and perhaps with arrogance. I was imperious in my disdain for what did not seem true. What was not "true" had no value. Truth for me was a synonym for Light. My "prayer mind," I was discovering with some surprise, was an anthology of biblical images of light. "Your light will rise like dawn out of darkness," Isaiah had promised; and again, "Arise, Jerusalem, rise clothed in light . . . the glory of the Lord shines over you." And the psalmist had assured me that "The Lord is my light and my salvation." And again, "In thy light we are bathed in light." Generations later the theme was repeated by John the Evangelist who bore witness to Jesus as the primal light: "The light shines on in the dark and the darkness has never mastered it," he promised.

I had never doubted that promise. It had kept me "true" in the darkness of doubt. I prayed for the grace to walk in light, to have my way illumined by truth. I wanted to be sure of my steps and sure of my words. *Claritas* was my passion. But now I was being led into a different land. The letters on a page of print had lost their hard focus, they were no longer clear and distinct. The edges were blurred no matter how faithfully I blinked.

Perhaps even had my vision not been diminished, in time age might have softened my inflexible passion for truth. Little by little I was learning that truth did not need to be as adamantine as I had demanded. Light need not always be incandescent. Shadows, with their soft blur, had a beauty which was gentle and accepting. Evening light, I was beginning to see, had its own truth.

ENCOUNTERS

# LEARNING GOD

It was mid-May and the conversation at lunch was turning on preparing first graders for First Communion and then on to our own memories: the anxious nuns, the first confession, the white veils, the interminable rehearsals. But here I was clearly out of the loop. I could remember nothing but my mother's horrified gasp when I spilled black ink on my new white shoes.

"I didn't go to Catholic school," I offered in explanation. No, I didn't go to CCD classes either. I don't remember any religious instruction. "But," came the question, "if you didn't get any instruction how did you know about God?" I floundered for an answer. I had never thought about it. My parents were Catholic, we went to church every Sunday but I could never remember any god-talk at home. We had no Catholic friends. There were no Catholic children in my school. The question seemed imponderable: how did I learn about God? For the first time I began to make a distinction between "learning about God" and "learning God," for I had not a moment's doubt that somehow in those early years I had learned God.

# LEARNING GOD

I can provide no evidence that this is true but there is truth beyond what we define as "evidence" and I know with certainty that in those remembered years the fact of God was something as certain as my own body. It was a god without definition. I could have told you nothing about him; I would have failed all the catechism questions. Perhaps if you had asked me I might have been able to say that "God was everywhere," but I'm not sure that even that was clear to me. I think there was one thing I knew – or perhaps "felt" is better: He was mine. God was mine. Only many years later did I start learning that I was his. Since there was no place in my life where he was talked about, I was free to make him up exactly as I needed him. Actually I had no sense of needing him since I had no sense of being without him. You only need your breath when you are running out of air.

But all of that was at the very beginning – the pre-history of my life. Looking back, trying to find an explanation, I have sometimes wondered if this is "the grace of baptism." I have never had much of a sense of baptism. I know it was something that happened to me but I have no material evidence of it. I have never seen my baptismal certificate. It seems that the church and its records were destroyed in a fire shortly after we moved so I have only the word of my parents that this auspicious event occurred. It was certainly auspicious because as I have been told there was a bit of a row between my father's children from his first marriage and members of my mother's family. (My mother was too ill to be present.) The result was that with some mutual concessions I was baptized "Florence" – a name that was never used and that I did not even know about until I was an adult. Nor am I sure of who my godparents were. In any event none of this has encouraged me to look back at my baptism as a happy moment when the waters washed over me making me "a child of God." It seemed more likely that I was being made the child of warring relatives.

And yet, was it this event, this sacramental moment, which had enabled me to "learn God?" Was there something beyond the muddle, the wrong-headed conflict between good people, which bathed me in light and irradiated not only that immaterial reality called my soul but the very veins of my body so that even my blood carried the presence of God? Perhaps. Why not? God, I have learned since, can pretty much do what He pleases. Since there was no one else to teach me "about" God, could not God teach me Himself?

I was six when we moved to Long Island and it was there in my new home that I made my First Communion. How I was prepared for this event I have no idea, certainly not by catechism classes. The church we went to each Sunday was, I discovered later, not an ordinary parish church but a "mission" church which was opened only on Sunday for an early morning Mass. It was a small white building situated on a little rise of land just outside the dismal little town of Setauket. Each Sunday Father Roex, a Dutch priest with a heavy accent and a perpetual scowl, opened the church and stood to welcome the meager congregation, mostly from the potato farms which extended beyond the town. In the winter he tried – not always successfully – to arrive early enough to start the furnace which gave more noise than heat. One icy Sunday I remember my father (much to my mother's embarrassment) stuffing a bill into the priest's hand – a bribe to encourage him to omit the sermon.

# LEARNING GOD

The church, as I remember it, had some twenty pews on each side, windows that hardly opened and an uncarpeted aisle leading to a makeshift altar. If there were statues I don't remember them. The pews were shiny and sticky with a heavy coat of shellac and in the hot weather they, along with the clothes of the parishioners, gave off a sweet cloying smell. What happened in that church I couldn't tell you. There was "the Mass," of course, but what that was exactly no one ever explained.

One thing I remember with disturbing clarity is the music. The music was provided by a stocky blond lady who always smelled of cigarettes. She sat high up in the small balcony in the back of the church and from there, every Sunday as we rose to leave, she belted out, accompanied by the wheezy organ, "Holy God we praise thy name." Her tobacco voice came slurring down from the organ loft in cascades of misdirected notes. Until I went to Catholic high school I never knew the Catholic Church had any more music to offer. "Holy God," as far as I was concerned, was the whole religious repertory. One of the greatest and most glorious parts of my college education was being introduced to the vast wealth of church music.

As far as I remember I made no connection between "church" and "God." I saw no conflict; I simply perceived two realities. One I embraced; the other I dismissed. But my confirmation came close to destroying even my private theology. This time there were instruction classes to attend. I secretly evaded them for weeks until the priest called my astonished parents asking for an explanation of my absence. The day of my confirmation was terrible. It took place in a strange church where I knew no one. I had the wrong kind of dress, and, being the tallest, I brought up the procession without a partner. To this day I don't know my confirmation name – and there are times when I wonder if the sacrament "took" – certainly it did not if my intention had anything to do with it.

My confirmation brought my life to a point of climax. The priest in charge – not the indifferent Father Roex – had found my attitude disturbing. I was woefully ignorant of my faith, he warned my parents. I needed instruction, I needed a Catholic environment. He would suggest a Catholic school and since there were none in the area he would suggest a boarding school where I would be guided and protected.

Thus, four months after my twelfth birthday, I began my high school career in the Academy of St. Joseph, Brentwood, Long Island, a "Select School for Young Ladies." It was under the auspices of the Sisters of St. Joseph and had a reputation for excellence. I started the year without resentment for being so rerouted, even with a certain eagerness to discover the mystery of being a Catholic. So far my education had consisted of one year of public school, followed by five years in a small, experimental school. It was an experience I thrived on. The entire enrollment was never over thirty. We had no classrooms, no teachers properly so-called; we had projects and mentors. We had no examinations and so no competition. With the help of our mentors, we learned on our own and at our own pace. For me it was a blissful process.

Brentwood, I soon discovered, was a "real" school. The number of children was, for me, overwhelming. Our first year class consisted of two sections with approximately twenty-five students in each. The total enrollment of the school reached about 275 students – all boarders – to be "guided and protected" as the good priest had promised.

There was no doubt that one would learn about religion here. The nuns were ubiquitous and for thirty-five minutes each day we were instructed in "religion." I had never spoken to a nun in my life and the only one I had seen was the black-robed person whom we passed when we went to New York City, sitting outside Pennsylvania Station with her begging cup. Now, for the first time, enclosed in an atmosphere of total religion, I was to learn "about" God.

I think it is true to say that I began with an "upright spirit" – a phrase Sister Marie Therese, our homeroom teacher, was fond of. I opened my ears and listened. I opened my eyes and read our textbook on the sacraments. It was all too much for my mind – too new, too different – and I foundered on the unfamiliar vocabulary. As for my heart – that I could not open. Whatever I was taught remained outside me. This god I was learning about was not a consoler, not a comforter. He had names and qualities and laws. He was a god of regulations and good behavior. He was omnipotent, omniscient, omnipresent. He had a son who was god, too, but also a human being. He was present everywhere but mostly confined in the beautiful gold box on the altar. I learned about God every day and yet I was shriveled up in loneliness. I was losing everything. My parents, my beautiful school, my friends, the limitless God who did not need to be defined and memorized.

When I went home for vacation – infrequently since school rules permitted few weekend breaks – the ache of knowing I had to return to my prison overwhelmed every joy being home provided. I was not a talker and I was not old enough to sort out my responses. My parents were happy that the reason they had sent me to boarding school was succeeding. I was learning about God; I was being "protected and guided." I had to admit even then that some of what surrounded my new religious experience intrigued me. "Holy God, we praise thy name," had expanded into a wealth of hymns, none of them very satisfying but at least a cut above Miss Purick's eternal rendition.

The chapel, as I learned to call it, was even to my untrained eyes very beautiful. It was immense and glorious compared to the musty little church of my home town. Every evening we were encouraged to "make a visit." A confusing term which everyone seemed to take for granted. But in time these evening "visits" became the cherished part of my life. It was the light which touched me and gave me back my God. The chandeliers, hung by golden chains from the high ceiling, were long ovals casting a light which softened the pews and the statues. The windows, carved alabaster, as Sister Marie Therese proudly explained, were translucent in the evening light. For a few short minutes the light and the silence brought me peace.

But those short evening intervals were not enough to save me. The rest of the day I pulled away from the unremitting regulations, the lessons which rarely deviated from the textbook, the gloom of uniforms. I watched the nuns who had nothing to reveal them except the oval of their faces. They carried themselves with grace but rarely smiled. (I hadn't yet learned the word "austere".) As I listened to Sister Marie Therese tabulate for us the attributes of God, I began to wonder if, as she taught us, God had really created her and shaped her or if she had created and shaped this intransigent divinity she revealed to us.

By the time I began my second year my "upright spirit" had been lost along with that sense of God which had supported and consoled me. I had begun to learn "about God." I was being "guided and protected" in my "faith." When, three years later, I received my high school diploma and my special medal which proclaimed me a "Child of Mary" all gods had gone. At the direction of our headmistress, who was concerned for my "religion," my parents had determined that I would go to a Catholic college for two years; when I was eighteen I could make my own choice.

Even now, after so many years to puzzle it out, I cannot provide – even for myself – an explanation of how I came to be what is called in church circles "a consecrated religious." That that is precisely what I am, I have no doubt; but who the god is to whom I have passionately consecrated my life still remains a mystery. When at the age of sixteen I started my freshman year at the College of New Rochelle in southern Westchester County I was hardly a candidate for anything but a troubled existence. Four years of loneliness had hardened me. I applied for a single room; I was not interested in friendship. I was interested in learning – on my own terms. As for God-talk, I was happy to discover that "religion" was a one credit course which met for an hour a week. The priest who gave it seemed no more interested in it than I did. It turned out to be a pleasant time to sit in the back of the lecture hall and write letters.

Yet little by little I began to crawl up out of my black hole. Friendship was part of it, widening vision was part of it, good books, good music, good conversation all played their part. And, of course, there was the simple act of growing beyond adolescence. None of this, however, fully explains the God-shift. There were evening "visits" here, too, but with a greater comprehension of who was there to be visited. I regained something of the god of inchoate presence who had comforted my childhood. He had now, as Shakespeare had said of invisible forces, "a local habitation and a name," although he was never restricted to these.

There was beauty, too. The beauty of the Bible, that limitlessly wonderful book of God's Word (and words). There was church music – there was Bach and the soaring wonder of the Glorias – Pulenc's and Vivaldi's. There were organ preludes shouting out the Resurrection and the tenderness of Christmas hymns. There was beauty, too, in the squandering richness of cathedrals and the austerity of monastic chapels. None of this was lost on me. I reveled in it. It countered the ugly poverty of our mission church with its sticky pews and slurring organ. But none of this was enough to explain the God-shift.

For a while it seemed that I had sacrificed one God for the other. That in my maturity I had learned to accept everything that was said "about" God. That the early God experience was subsumed in this newly learned divinity. I know now that this isn't true. There is still so much of the learned God which seems irrelevant to me. Theology has always seemed to me a terrifying science: so many words to explain what in my mind seems to me essentially inexplicable.

I had come to God by a different way. The angle of my perception had determined what I saw of God. It was not that

# LEARNING GOD

I had experienced a different god but I had not come to him by talk "about" him, by explanations, by church rituals. I no longer dismiss these things. I have learned to accept them as part of the way God reaches us. But I know they will never be for me what they are for my companions. The "sacraments" and all the explanations about them still escape me. It's not a question of rejecting them but of being bewildered by them. I listen to passionate discussions about "the Church" and what it calls us to. I know I am a member of this church and that in some mysterious way I am "saved" in it and by it. And yet it all seems far, far away; nothing that touches my own passion for God. Who, I sometimes wonder, was the God I made my vows to? I don't think I know. And does it matter? Not to God, I am sure.

I have a fantasy about my death. In that final moment of consciousness the God I "learned" and the God I "learned about" will converge. Whatever truth there is in each will coalesce into that Perfect One and in that blinding moment of eternity I will know the truth.

Breinigsville, PA USA
12 February 2010
232341BV00001B/74/P